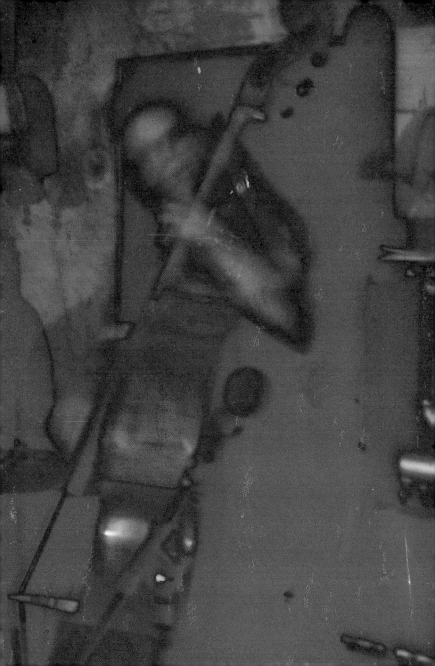

CONTENTS

THE STORY OF JAZZ
BOP AND BEYOND

Frank Bergerot and Arnaud Merlin

DISCOVERIES

HARRY N. ABRAMS, INC., PUBLISHERS

Evolved in part from spirituals sung by slaves, jazz is the only truly American musical form. It was created by blacks, for blacks. For years, it was considered to be mere entertainment, but with the advent of bebop in the 1940s, young jazz musicians joined the avant-garde: Bop opened the door to modern jazz, the privileged expression of a growing number of artists, strangers to its origins.

CHAPTER I
WHAT TO MAKE OF BEBOP?

Charlie Parker (opposite, on the sax) with pianist, composer, and teacher Lennie Tristano and others in 1949.

In the clubs of Manhattan's 52nd Street, small experimental bebop groups revolutionized jazz. At the time, New York was the capital of the artistic avant-garde, of intellectual excitement. Literature, theater, and painting were being enthusiastically discussed in the city's living rooms.

Recently arrived in New York to rally for the cause of bebop, the arranger Gil Evans, however, did not have a living room. One simple room near 52nd Street was enough for him, and it attracted a crowd, day and night. The leaders of black music gathered around a turntable there, playing recordings of sax players Lester Young and Charlie Parker as well as such European composers as Alban Berg and Maurice Ravel. They met in that room to listen and to talk with each other—and with young white musicians as well.

By the 1940s jazz was no longer the exclusive property of the African-American community. Bop made jazz into a language accessible to all musicians and music lovers in search of a well-informed mode of expression that was freer and more physical than Western classical music.

Birth of the Cool

Cool means fresh and refreshing but also, of course, relaxed. To someone who's getting upset, you say, "Keep cool." In the late 1940s white jazz musicians began to interpret Charlie Parker's jazz in a new, "cool" way—and the name stuck. But, paradoxically, the beginnings of cool are attributed to the boldest of the black musicians, Miles Davis. Indeed, his 1949 recordings for Capitol Records are so significant in this regard that later reissues

Gil Evans rushed to New York's 52nd Street (above) as soon as he arrived in 1946. He found a one-room apartment nearby. The activity of what was then called The Street was reaching its peak at the time. In 1948 Miles Davis' nonet performed at the Royal Roost on Broadway.

were grouped under the title *Birth of the Cool*.

Compared to Dizzy Gillespie, the other all-star trumpet player of the period, Miles Davis lacked both virtuosity and a brilliant tone. Yet he created a sober, airy, reflective style all his own featuring a quiet resonance, avoiding high notes, and favoring the medium register. "Keep cool!" he seemed to say to Dizzy Gillespie's velocity, mimicking the message Lester Young seemed to convey to the impetuous Coleman Hawkins. But he wasn't satisfied with the rapid unison phrases and the unbridled solos that characterized bebop. In 1948, when Davis formed an ensemble,

Miles Davis, Lee Konitz, and Gerry Mulligan (left to right) recording *Birth of the Cool* for Capitol Records.

he tried something new: Instead of the usual bebop quintet, he formed a nine-piece band, a nonet.

And then he called on arrangers Gil Evans and Gerry Mulligan. The band featured Davis' trumpet—along with two saxophones, a trombone, a rhythm section, and two instruments rarely used in jazz until then, a French horn and a tuba. (The tuba had been used in the rhythm section of the first jazz ensembles in New Orleans, but had been largely replaced by the string bass by this time.)

Evans, Mulligan, and Davis

Whereas in some bands there was a very clear musical separation between the trumpets, trombones, and saxophones, Gil Evans preferred the density and the richness obtained by fusing their varied tones in his arrangements. His orchestrations evoke the shimmer of colors and the weight of fabrics. The seduction of the sound took precedence, and his "Moon Dreams" stretched itself out in dramatic torpor.

Among the other arrangers Miles Davis worked with for the occasion, all of them regulars at Gil Evans' room, baritone sax player Gerry Mulligan was particularly innovative: He made deliberate efforts to break with the traditional eight-measure form. When the harmonic structure still referred to this convention, he would shift his orchestrations to mask it. More importantly, in the introduction to the theme of "Jeru," he called the sovereignty of the four-beat measure and rhythmic unity into

Prestige Records (which released the album above) illustrated some of the new concepts of jazz through pieces by Stan Getz, Gerry Mulligan, Miles Davis (in his first session for long-playing records), and the Lee Konitz Sextet (on a legendary album entitled *Ezz-thetic,* based on a futuristic composition by George Russell).

Below: Gil Evans and Miles Davis, whose collaboration after *Birth of the Cool* never ended.

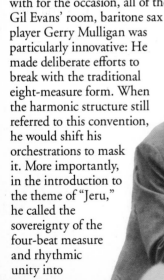

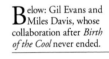

question with isolated two- and three-beat measures.

Miles Davis' nonet went against all the then-current ideas about the lightweight quality of jazz. It seemed to demand the kind of listening one would expect in Carnegie Hall, not a noisy club.

The alto sax player Lee Konitz, one of the principal soloists Miles Davis invited to the 1949 Capitol Records sessions, seemed an unlikely candidate for his major role. He was to the bebop saxophone what Woody Allen is to American cinema (the recent scandals notwithstanding): He had the pallor of an

Baritone sax player Gerry Mulligan (above) was one of the arrangers for Miles Davis' nonet on the *Birth of the Cool* recordings.

Left: The "Four Brothers," three tenors and a baritone—or Stan Getz (also below), Al Cohn, Zoot Sims, and Serge Chaloff—here accompanied by Sam Marowitz. While these players were not related, they were a true brotherhood of white West Coast followers of Lester Young.

absentminded student, in sharp contrast to the exuberant faces of bebop. The same was true of his playing. He softened Charlie Parker's virtuosity with the influence of the floating phrases of Lester Young and Lennie Tristano.

Piano player Tristano contributed a theoretical foundation to the discoveries of bop musicians and spread their ideas through his teaching. Emphasizing melody, harmony, and rhythm, he stream-lined bop's expressionistic aspects. The coterie of young white musicians he assembled,

particularly sax players Lee Konitz and Warne Marsh, tempered bop's dazzling language by adopting airy resonances and vibratoless tones. Referring to the fugues and counterpoints of Johann Sebastian Bach, these musicians loved to do two-part improvisations and, with Lennie Tristano, were responsible for the first free improvisations (without any written theme or even any agreed-upon harmonic pattern).

Cool Crystallized on the West Coast

In the forties Stan Kenton, originally from the West Coast, combined swing with the spirit of 20th-century European composers. While it may have contributed to the frequent bombast of his work, his

Lee Konitz and Warne Marsh belonged to the school of Lennie Tristano. Tristano's coldness and the intellectuality of his approach were criticized —it wasn't always understood that his first concern was with inner attention, reciprocal listening, enduring imagination, and true discourse removed from the routine formulas.

training served as a crucible for West Coast jazz. Indeed, it was in California that the principal players—Art Pepper, Gerry Mulligan, Zoot Sims, Shorty Rogers, Shelly Manne, and Frank Rosolino —met, all of them white, and all of them equally fascinated by Charlie Parker and Lester Young.

From 1947 on Woody Herman made the "Four Brothers" famous by putting the four unrelated sax players (three tenors and a baritone) at the center of this band. The best known of the "brothers" will always be Stan Getz. Discovered because of his solo in "Early Autumn" in 1948, he set himself up as the apostle of the fragility and romanticism that typified the West Coast style.

Even though the majority of the West Coasters emerged from the ranks of Stan Kenton's and Woody Herman's big bands, it would be dangerous to reduce this style to a single current. Before anything else, it

The lighthouse at Hermosa Beach, California, was the gathering place for the West Coasters. They came together often around the club's programmer, the bassist Howard Rumsey, who conducted his All Stars there.

was a question of a geographic place where young musicians came together, more attracted by the gentle California life-style than by the hard edges of New York. Technically able musicians, they found work in Hollywood studios and shared a taste for the subtlety and writing style that they had developed under the influence of Miles Davis' nonet.

The West Coast and World-Weariness

As much as New York bebop seemed to be the expression of a community struggling for survival and recognition, so West Coast jazz musicians seemed to give themselves fully to introspection and existential suffering, combined with an indifference to everything around them. Admirers and critics alike found it difficult to place these young, white, middle-class people on the same level as their urban black idols.

In the fifties, as McCarthy's campaign against Communism progressed and the United States plunged into the cold war, cultural life was at a peak. The anti-establishment writers of the Beat generation often referred to jazz in their work and participated with the California musicians in experiments combining music and literature. Preceding rock and roll, West Coast jazz was the expression of a youth in rebellion against the middle class from which it came.

Far from being easygoing, the music of alto saxophonist Paul Desmond, for example, transmitted a quiet and embittered desperation, while Art Pepper, more unstable and intense, displayed an insatiable sensuality on the same instrument. As for Chet Baker, he was the great romantic figure

From the look of this trumpet-playing frogman, who appeared on the cover of an album that brought together all the main California musicians, one would have the impression of a lighthearted music, a music to relax by after a day at the beach. However, West Coast jazz was a very different thing, as the experiments of the trio of Shelly Manne, Jimmy Giuffre, and Shorty Rogers demonstrated.

of the West Coast. He played trumpet in a pianoless quartet led by Gerry Mulligan, who exemplified the spirit of the California fifties. This quartet was concerned with structure and melodic clarity, and its solos for two voices in counterpoint, sweet atmosphere, and feeling of chamber music foreshadowed many of the avenues explored in later jazz. Finally, the absence of the piano and the statement of the harmonies by the double bass alone offered wider freedom for the soloist.

Despite the indelible impression made by the Miles Davis nonet, West Coast music may have seemed true to the image conveyed by California beaches: sunny and carefree. But the apparent easiness hid a fundamentally disciplined innovative spirit.

Among the names in California jazz, the trumpet player Shorty Rogers was prominent. Combining the colors of the Miles Davis nonet with the spontaneous and "swinging" writing of Count Basie's middle years,

Art Pepper + Eleven is typical of the West Coast style: by the musicians who produced it (Pete Candoli, Jack Sheldon, Bud Shank, Bill Perkins, Richie Kamuca, Russ Freeman, and Mel Lewis), by the reference to East Coast bop (compositions by Dizzy Gillespie, Charlie Parker, and Thelonious Monk), and, finally, by the magnificence of the sound shared by California arrangers. The paradox of the West Coast resides in this recording, somewhere between the Hollywood studios, where some musicians were earning comfortable salaries, and the prison of San Quentin, where Art Pepper paid for his life as a junkie.

Left: Dave Brubeck, who studied with Darius Milhaud, developed outside of the California community with a few partners— Bill Smith, Joe Morello, and Paul Desmond, composer of the famous "Take Five," an extreme example of West Coast jazz.

Shorty Rogers also borrowed from the sophisticated structures of classical music.

These borrowings were legal currency on the West Coast. Dave Brubeck's quartet popularized a number of processes foreign to jazz in this manner and encountered widespread success—so much so that even today he remains suspect in the eyes of purists.

The experiments of the saxophone and clarinet player Jimmy Giuffre during the fifties, however, were far more radical. With an unusual ensemble —clarinet, trumpet, and drums—he anticipated the liberties taken by "free jazz" in the sixties. His taste for the intimate atmosphere of chamber music made him the precursor of the options that bloomed in the seventies.

With a face like James Dean's, a relaxed style, and a purified lyricism, trumpet player Chet Baker (left) was first dismissed as a pale imitator of Miles Davis. Later he was recognized as one of the most astounding improvisers since Louis Armstrong.

With its famous penguins, the album cover of *The Three & the Two* by the drummer Shelly Manne is a collectors' item today. This experimental music played on the preoccupations of pianist John Lewis, arranger for Dizzy Gillespie's big band and Miles Davis' nonet. Lewis revisited the canonic forms of classical music with his Modern Jazz Quartet (album cover below) and created the "third stream" with composer Gunther Schuller. This third stream merged the spontaneity of jazz with the forms of classical music.

Right: Dexter Gordon, who developed his own unique way of assimilating Lester Young's lessons in cool.

West Coast and Cool Jazz Were Not the Exclusive Property of White Musicians

In Hollywood the sublime duels of the black saxophone players Dexter Gordon and Wardell Gray were recorded in June 1947. They shared the cult of Lester Young with their white colleagues, but their sound was more expressionistic, the flow of their phrases more consistent with the demands of bebop, and their intention more aggressive. When they gave themselves fully to the indolence of phrasing "like Lester," they did so with much more sensuality.

On the other hand, other black musicians, on the West Coast and elsewhere, developed a taste for muffled and refined tones. When "hard bop," which arose in the 1950s, was at its hottest, Miles Davis was continuing to cultivate a restrained cool style of playing. What he obtained, however, was not so much an effect of relaxation as an impression of controlled violence that would provoke a feeling of tension in the listener.

While cool was gaining popularity on the West Coast, the black musicians on the East Coast were active, too. They made bop accessible to the large ensemble, enriched its forms, mastered its vocabulary, and became apprentices to new rhythms. By the mid-fifties, they had developed a hardened tone, drawing from blues and gospel in order to preserve the specific characteristics of African-American music.

CHAPTER II
TOWARD HARD BOP AND MODAL JAZZ

Miles Davis (left) and Thelonious Monk (right): Two exceptional figures who bore witness to the richness of African-American music in the mid-fifties.

The trumpet player Dizzy Gillespie started his career in big bands and did not hesitate to let the first sounds of bebop be heard there, sometimes under the glare of his bandleaders. In 1946 he formed his own big band, in which some of the best-known names played, and he created a sensation by incorporating Afro-Cuban elements into his music. Indeed, contacts between American jazz musicians and those hailing from Cuba and Puerto Rico—many of whom had been in New York since the thirties—multiplied in this decade. In this way, jazz musicians broadened their rhythmic habits and explored new ways of expressing the beat.

Big Band Bebop

With Dizzy Gillespie's big band, especially on "Cubana Be" and "Cubana Bop," the revolutionary nature of bebop language exploded on a wider scale. In his quest for modernity Dizzy Gillespie chose his collaborators judiciously. Among them, Tadd Dameron created a sensation. A composer-arranger trained in the school of swing, Dameron allied himself very early with the bebop aesthetic through the daring of such tunes as "Hot House." He begrudged his white colleagues on the West Coast nothing. Gladly citing French composer Maurice Ravel among his influences, he attached equal importance to the resonant beauty of the whole and to the melodic quality of each part, at a time when

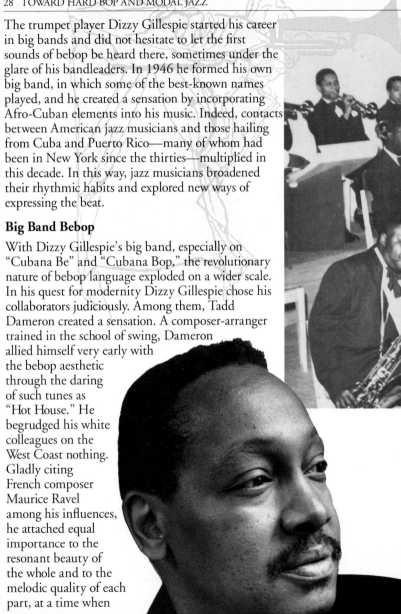

many others were concerned only with the lead voice.

Dameron's skill in preserving melody through even the most "distorted" harmonies was shared by one of his closest friends, trumpet player Fats Navarro. A soloist who used his uncommon imagination to avoid the harmonic traps of bebop, Navarro chiseled melodic lines of such density and pertinence that they were a decisive influence on future generations.

Dizzy Gillespie's big band (above) made use of a new generation of arrangers: Gil Fuller, George Russell, John Lewis, Chico O'Farrill, and Tadd Dameron (opposite). Dameron's work had a litheness that prefigured the character of today's big bands.

Monk's "Gap"

During the 1950s Miles Davis continued to make an impact; in fact, he had never stopped asserting himself as one of the major voices of bebop since *Birth of the Cool*. In contrast, pianist-composer Thelonious Monk, a master improviser, remained little understood.

On 24 December 1954 the two came together in a recording studio. Davis had a hard time falling in with Monk's strange harmonies, and finally he told the piano player to be quiet during his solos, preferring to rely solely on the double bass, which provided him with more space.

Was what happened on the second take of "The Man I Love" due to Thelonious Monk's frustration? His solo began as they so often did, with an elongated deconstruction of the theme, in this case by George Gershwin. Then the rhythmic shifts and unexpected dissonances multiplied, so much so

Like their pre-war predecessors, bop musicians were a hit in France. Above: The album *Bud Powell in Paris,* recorded in 1963. Below: Tommy Potter, Boris Vian, Kenny Dorham, Juliette Gréco, Miles Davis, Michèle Vian, and Charlie Parker in 1949.

that listeners have the feeling of a staircase giving way beneath their feet. Suddenly, a long silence set in: Monk stopped playing. Out of patience, Miles Davis started playing his trumpet to fill the void—upon which the pianist, coming out of his torpor, immediately threw himself on the keyboard to take the floor again.

Much has been said about this "gap" of Monk's, though no one knows precisely what happened between the two men. However, the incident does illuminate these fundamental figures of bebop. Thelonious Monk, a misunderstood modern hermit, threw his harmonies on the piano the way one throws a match on an explosive. Each new combination seemed to plunge him into intense thought, out of which

Fats Navarro (above) said of his colleagues: "They don't know chord progressions. When they know them better, when they're comfortable with them, maybe then we will have made truly modern jazz." It is through him and Clifford Brown, whom he influenced, that the modernity of Charlie Parker's message became completely assimilated.

the next harmony would emerge. He died in 1982, after a silence of years, and yet his compositions are among the most frequently played today. The eccentricity of his playing has remained a touchpoint for each new generation breaking with the conventions of the moment.

Thelonious Monk was not the first pianist condemned to silence during Miles Davis' solos. The way in which Davis distributed the roles and the order of instrumental entrances in his pieces came straight out of the theater. He managed the time constraints of a long-playing record as a true director, multiplying the internal arrangements or modifying the atmosphere with his mute. He never hesitated to have the lights in a studio turned off to put his musicians in a particular mood. Whether he was with the arrangers of *Birth of the Cool* or the young musicians of his quintet, Miles was always a great dramatist.

"I just didn't like what he played behind *me*.... See, you had to play like Coltrane to play with Monk—all that space and disjointed s—— he used to play."

Miles Davis,
*Miles, the
Autobiography,* 1989

These many enrichments of the early material of bop among black or white musicians insured that, despite Charlie Parker's death in 1955, there would be a definite future for this music. It would be relaunched with hard bop.

The Beginning of "Black Is Beautiful"

In 1954 Senator Joseph McCarthy's "witch-hunt" was repudiated by the Senate, and the United States moved toward a relatively liberal period. Under the influence of Martin Luther King, Jr., who preached nonviolence, African-Americans found a faith in their struggle against racism. To their demand for integration was added the demand for the right to be different. "Blackness" began to be lived with pride, and the late-sixties slogan "Black is Beautiful" was already present in the minds of many.

In the middle of the fifties, the trumpet player Clifford Brown could be seen as the perfect incarnation of this beauty. Stylistic heir to Fats Navarro, he stunningly articulated his phrases, with a fabulously limpid melodic sense, in spite of the complex harmonic detours with which his compositions were strewn. His style, sharp as a blade, was the complete opposite of the introspective, lighthearted, and experimental tone of West Coast jazz. In this way Clifford Brown laid the groundwork for hard bop. Sadly, he would die too soon to enjoy the effects of his own contributions.

Hard Bop: A Return to Blues and Gospel

Having invaded the market during the first half of the fifties, cool jazz tempted certain black artists with its sophistication and restraint. It spurred the next new wave—hard bop, which featured loud, full-voiced instrumental sound and emotional

While Monk and Miles were recording together for Prestige on 24 December 1954, Clifford Brown (left) was improvising for the singer Helen Merrill on the theme "What's New," a melody that is counted among the masterpieces of jazz history. In the same year—with the drummer Art Blakey and the pianist Horace Silver— he had participated in the first performances by the Jazz Messengers, who were to become the leaders of hard bop. At the time of the car accident that was to cost him his life, Clifford Brown was associated with the drummer Max Roach, heading a quintet that included saxophone player Sonny Rollins. Even today, few trumpet players can escape his influence, especially apparent in the early records of Wynton Marsalis.

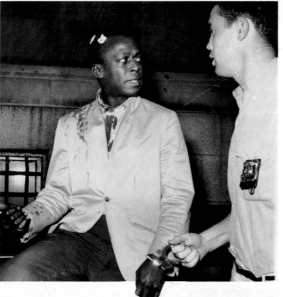

Senator Joseph McCarthy (above) in front of the map showing the expansion of the Communist party in the United States. The "witch-hunt" extended to any community suspect in the eyes of reactionary America. The decline of McCarthyism, however, changed little in the treatment of African-Americans. On 26 August 1959 Miles Davis was violently apprehended by the police (left) for refusing to "keep moving" in front of Birdland, where he was working.

performances. It was the opportunity for musicians to return to the roots of African-American music, blues and gospel, but it was also their opportunity to renew their ties with black audiences, baffled by the avant-gardist aspects of modern jazz.

The craze for rhythm and blues was at its peak, and suddenly everyone was talking about soul. Through this music the black community proudly displayed its cultural and spiritual differences, distinguishing itself from American puritanism by reconciling body and soul, dance and religious trances, sexual ecstasy, and mystical heights. Soul music became the profane rejoinder to the music of the black churches: It addressed the dancer and spoke of love.

Blues March

In coming back to the forms of the blues or the spiritual, jazz became "churchy." Certain titles were

Since the forties the term *rhythm and blues* encompassed all of black American popular music, but in the fifties, soul, a reference to the growing influence of the spiritual and gospel song, took over. It was only a small step from prayer meetings in black churches to soul music, from the art of preachers and gospel singers to that of James Brown, Aretha Franklin, or Ray Charles. The psychedelic feeling of the poster on the right testifies to the interest that the pop music audience in the sixties showed in soul.

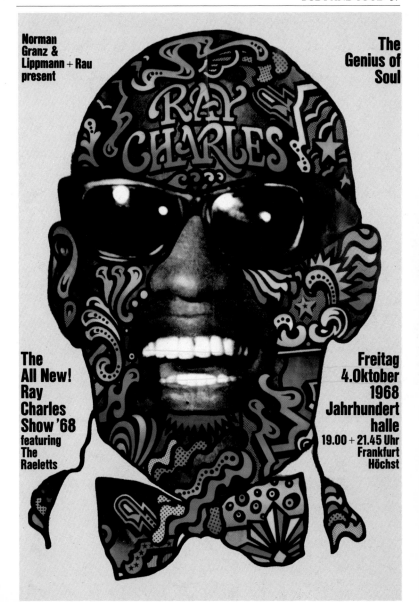

Norman
Granz &
Lippmann + Rau
present

The
Genius of
Soul

RAY
CHARLES

The
All New!
Ray
Charles
Show '68
featuring
The
Raeletts

Freitag
4.Oktober
1968
Jahrhundert
halle
19.00 + 21.45 Uhr
Frankfurt
Höchst

entirely unambiguous: *The Sermon, The Preacher,
Prayer Meeting*. But there was also funk (a word
derived from slang allusions to bodily odors). Close to
physical pleasures, simple, direct, peremptory, and
blatantly joyous, hard bop, feeding off both of these
currents, was the expression of a proud black
community, sure of the outcome of its struggles. To
be convinced all you have to do is listen to Benny
Golson's compositions for Art Blakey—such as "Blues
March," "Moanin'," or "Along Came Betty"—or

Horace Silver (left) first won renown playing with Stan Getz and Miles Davis (poster below). Musical leader of the Jazz Messengers when they began in 1954, he was replaced by Art Blakey in 1956. It was at that time that he became the pianist of funk par excellence. The rhythmic efficiency of his accompaniments, the inexorable progression of his phrases, the simplicity of his statements, and the "gospelizing" accents of his compositions breathed into his quintets that mixture of triviality and lightness that characterizes hard bop. Trumpet players Blue Mitchell, Woody Shaw, Kenny Dorham, Randy Brecker, and Tom Harrell and saxophone players Hank Mobley, Junior Cook, Joe Henderson, Michael Brecker, and Larry Schneider were among the celebrities who played in these quintets.

Horace Silver's themes—"Song for My Father" or "Nica's Dream."

Endowed with a vital energy, the drummer Art Blakey led the Jazz Messengers, the beacon group of hard bop. Blakey discovered many talents: Wayne Shorter, Freddie Hubbard, Keith Jarrett, and dozens of others—and, in effect, conducted their apprenticeships in hard bop.

The indelible message was about the importance of the rhythm section. In early bop the rhythm section simply stated the chords and maintained the tempo, offering a stimulating contrast to the soloist. In hard bop, however, its task was to establish the atmosphere, according to repetitive formulas inspired by gospel and soul music. Rhythmic arrangements provoked dancers into swaying. As in rhythm and blues music, the hard bop beat relied strongly on syncopation in traditional four-beat measures. But even four-beat measures no longer had the exclusivity they'd had since the twenties, as the three-part division became more and more frequently used: In fact, it is related to the very definition of swing, the essence of African-American music.

Binary Phrasing and Latin Jazz

Swing guaranteed flexibility, dynamics, and rhythmic richness in jazz. It introduced subjectivity and emotion to an art based on regularity. It was the key to the freedom with which jazz players placed each one of their notes. Up to that point swing had been related to the asymmetry of ternary phrasing, a term referring to a three-part division not only of the measure but of time in general. Where the classical musician played two equal notes, the jazz player would stretch the first and rush the second, thus

BiNARY phraseing —

A rt Blakey (left) and accompanied by Lee Morgan, Wayne Shorter, Curtis Fuller, and Reggie Workman (opposite). Among the drummers who were his contemporaries and must be remembered particularly are Max Roach, Roy Haynes, and Philly Joe Jones.

O verleaf: The conga player Candido Camero. The symmetry of hands beating Cuban drums corresponds to the equal subdivisions of the beat in Afro-Cuban music. During the fifties, this style—no longer as exotic seeming as it had been with Dizzy Gillespie—was now integrated into the vocabulary of the jazz musician. With Art Blakey African polyrhythms were rediscovered and all rhythmic habits of African-American music came into play.

creating an impression of elasticity, of rebound. Binary phrasing made a timid entrance into Gillespie's jazz, with the symmetric drumming on the skins of Afro-Cuban drums. But, after concluding that "it swung" as much in two as in three, jazz musicians assimilated more and more new rhythmic habits. Starting at the end of the fifties, Latin rhythms (Jamaican calypso, Afro-Cuban mambo, Brazilian bossa nova) were no longer just exotic borrowings but a real part of the everyday vocabulary of jazz musicians; they were a major contribution to the success of hard bop.

The succinct arrangements for several voices magnified the efficiency of the themes even more. These themes were often inspired by blues or gospel, whose typical formulas they emphasized. Instead of transforming the standards of musical comedy through complex plagiarism, as the bop players had done until then, hard bop players avoided them and often favored their own compositions—sparser and characterized by a certain brutality, both harmonic and rhythmic—instead.

The rapid chord changes in bebop imposed constant melodic divergences upon the soloists. With time, they learned to convey a general view of these changes while preserving the continuity of their phrases. Hard bop still linked chords without any apparent relationship but no longer weighed itself down with complex developments

E ven though he became one of the great figures of modern jazz after playing with Miles Davis and Max Roach, Sonny Rollins (right and below) did not stop looking for his place among the great innovators. However, from 1957 on, his different trios (saxophone, bass, drums) with the drummers Pete LaRoca and Elvin Jones (*A Night at the Village Vanguard*), Max Roach (*The Freedom Suite*), or Shelly Manne (*Way Out West*) marked the epoch by the freedom of expression allowed by the piano's absence.

used to justify these inconsistencies. The same chord could last for several measures, during which the soloist would have all the time needed to structure a melodic improvisation, invent unprecedented rhythmic formulas, prepare the arrival of the next chord, and conceive of an atmosphere that would preside over the dramatic profile of the entire solo.

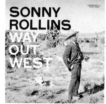

"Peace Piece"

Bill Evans

The white face of Bill Evans stands out among the players of hard bop. It was under the fingers of this young pianist that some of the hottest preoccupations of the moment were crystallized. When, on 15 December 1958, he recorded "Peace Piece" as an unaccompanied piano solo, he pushed his taste for spareness to the extreme. In it, he improvised on two endlessly repeated chords for almost seven minutes. Concentrating on such minimalism, he explored the scale corresponding to these chords, but not without taking the liberty to wander off into neighboring scales.

In doing so, he drew on the teachings of composer George Russell, whose theories, found in his "Lydian Chromatic Concept of Tonal Organization," offered a new approach to jazz musicians. Rather than contend with the increasingly elaborate chord changes required by fifties jazz, a modal approach (based on the notes in one scale) offered new simplicity. Modal jazz, often inspired by non-European musical forms, became widespread in the sixties. On the one hand, with modal jazz and the blossoming of a new lyricism harmonic language would be reborn; on the other, it would find its own negation in the upcoming explosion of free jazz.

It was through his contact with George Russell (below left) that Bill Evans (right) began his use of modes. With his compositions "Cubana Be" and "Cubana Bop" for Dizzy Gillespie's big band, George Russell confirmed his desire to free himself from the customary harmonic progressions. He took advantage of a hospital stay (for tuberculosis) to write his "Lydian Chromatic Concept of Tonal Organization," a theoretic prelude to modal jazz, which he put into practice during the course of his exciting career as a bandleader.

"So here we stand, on the edge of Hell, in Harlem, and wonder what we will do, in the face of all that we remember"

Langston

John Coltrane was the master of modern jazz in the early sixties. He was a leader for angry young black musicians who wanted to reappropriate their music from the dominant white culture. Against a background of the civil rights movement, jazz musicians rejected the aesthetic criteria of mainstream American society and invented something new that would be called free jazz.

CHAPTER III
THE ROAD TO FREEDOM

In Archie Shepp's apartment (left). Charles Mingus (below) was harshly critical of free jazz, less for its content than for its achievements.

The saxophone player John Coltrane was a calm, reserved, contemplative man, completely absorbed by his music and, even more, by the philosophical and mystical problems he sought to solve through his music. Although annoyed by Coltrane's incessant questions, Miles Davis asked him to join his quintet in 1956. Perhaps he understood that one of the great figures of jazz would emerge from these interrogations. From his first steps with Davis until his death, Coltrane never stopped questioning his art.

With Giant Steps

In 1957, during a stint at the Five Spot in New York City with the Thelonious Monk Quartet, Coltrane was inspired by the unusual piano accompaniments. When Monk would leave the stage, Coltrane would take advantage of this time to explore new harmonic processes during long improvisations.

In 1958 Coltrane joined Miles Davis' new sextet, which recorded his masterpiece, *Kind of Blue*, a year later. Coltrane's playing had changed: From this point on he produced absolute torrents of sound. He brought his reflections on chord progressions to an end while recording "Giant Steps," the ultimate outcome of the harmonic system of bebop, with his quartet. Thereafter he pursued his quest in the direction of modal jazz. In the meantime, even side by side with Miles Davis, he became increasingly alienated, and his long solo flights seemed to come from another universe.

The Ascension

After listening to various musicians, Coltrane put his dream quartet together in 1961. With the solid double bassist Jimmy Garrison as pivotal figure, the drummer Elvin Jones developed a polyrhythm that implied, rather than stated, the tempo; and onto this tumultuous undertow McCoy Tyner's piano repeated

After his first recordings (above: *Blue Train,* Blue Note, 1957), John Coltrane sought to escape from the harmonic system of bebop. In his contact with the modal options of Bill Evans and Miles Davis (notably in *Kind of Blue,* 1959), he glimpsed the solutions that would lead him in 1961 to put together his famous quartet with McCoy Tyner, Jimmy Garrison (opposite), and Elvin Jones.

tireless motifs that lured the soloist into a trance. Tyner's intentional harmonic uncertainties invited Coltrane to multiply the melodic phrases. One mode followed another, mixed, ground down, saturated with notes jostling each other until they overlapped, for a "multiphonic" effect. Occasionally the tempo even disappeared altogether, diluted in long incantatory recitatives, such as the last section of *Love Supreme*. More and more often, Coltrane preferred to omit the piano and the double bass and remain alone with the energy flow transmitted by Elvin Jones.

Some young members of the avant-garde of free jazz, who worshiped Coltrane, were invited to participate in the recording of the influential album *Ascension*, and one of them, Pharoah Sanders (tenor sax), began to play with him regularly after that. Soon Coltrane rid himself of McCoy Tyner's piano, which he had begun to see as standing in his way.

Elvin Jones left, too, in reaction to the arrival of the drummer Rashied Ali, whose conceptions of free jazz he did not share. Coltrane died on 17 July 1967, finally having attained the end of his quest for the upper limits of both fame and music. Throngs of musicians of every type remain haunted by the influence of his work to this day.

Ornette Coleman, Herald

At the end of the fifties, however, Ornette Coleman's star rose higher than John Coltrane's. This young saxophone player from the West Coast had already rejected the harmonic aspect of Charlie Parker's legacy: He wanted to retain only its essence. "Let's play the music and not its background," he declared. To him technique was secondary; in his eyes only the feeling and authenticity of expression counted. The

Coltrane's album *Om* (top) and Pharoah Sanders' *Tauhid*. Coltrane and McCoy Tyner (below). Coltrane's post-1966 band (opposite).

lyricism of his melodic playing was startling and, paradoxically, elusive.

The "harmolodic theory" he was to develop over the years escaped musicologists' understanding; it came from philosophic—better yet, poetic— rather than from technical concerns. His art was reminiscent of the authenticity of slaves' "field hollers," which outside observers have never managed to describe in the vocabulary of European musicology.

The forms he borrowed made frequent reference to blues or structures inherited from musical comedy, but his "Blues Connotation" in eleven and a half bars is more evocative of the uncertainties of the early blues players than of the academic twelve-bar blues.

Many bop musicians took offense at these ideas, which put their entire mode of thinking into question. However, the support Ornette Coleman received from John Lewis and some West Coast musicians allowed him to record his first disks. They looked like a manifesto: *Something Else!*, *Tomorrow Is the Question*, and *The Shape of Jazz to Come*. On 21 December 1960 he made a recording with a double quartet. The new formula

S axophone player and composer Ornette Coleman (below) rejected the logic of Western harmony. In his eyes, the only things that counted were the wandering flow of melodic inspiration and the beat, free of every metric concern. His album *Free Jazz* is illustrated above.

marked the beginning of an epoch: The new album was called *Free Jazz*, relating to the intention of drawing form and musicality from the apparent chaos he presented. To most musicians—and the public—Coleman's music did sound like chaos.

"The New Thing"

Was free jazz really jazz? At first they called it "the new thing." This new jazz was "free" not only in the sense that the first improvisations were free. It also claimed to be free of the very definitions of jazz and even the art of music as formulated by critics (primarily from the white culture). "It is our music" is indeed what Ornette Coleman's album *This Is Our Music* stated in protest, echoing the new black thinkers who challenged the right of whites to hold forth on a music that was not their own. The criteria

Despite the elimination of the piano, Coleman and Don Cherry (above) still turned back to bebop. But their goal was less to maintain a perfect ensemble than to create a dynamic and spontaneous relationship between their two instruments.

of beauty, purity of sound, virtuosity, logical form, and so on—which had defined music up to now— all moved to the background. Going back to the first African-American songs, free jazz even went so far as to renounce rhythmic regularity and swing, practically the definition of jazz. All it retained were the fundamental elements that distinguish black American music—energy, involvement of the body, raw sound, and improvisation (in other words, a "lightness of being," to borrow Milan Kundera's expression, that favors the moment, the immediate, the temporary). By extension, free jazz expressed an interest in world music—Arab, Oriental, and, of course, African.

With African dress (opposite, Pharoah Sanders) and musical exoticism, black musicians paid homage to Mother Africa.

Free Jazz, a Mirror of the Civil Rights Movement

The history of free jazz corresponds to the history of the civil rights movement: the rise of demands under Martin Luther King, Jr., and other, more radical, leaders; the explosion of the black ghettos; the struggles led by the Black Panthers; the solidarity with the liberation movements of the Third World; repression, marginalization, ferment. In its political involvement, free jazz questioned Western art's ambition to raise itself above the material world. On these grounds, it had its place on university campuses during the uprisings of the late sixties, and it excited new criticism from white people. These white critics proved to be as intolerant and sectarian as lovers of old jazz styles.

HE HOUSE OF COMMON SENSE
ME OF PROPER PROPAGANDA.

WORLD HISTORY
BOOK OUTLET ON

2,000,000,000
(TWO BILLION)
AFRICANS AND NON-WHITE PEOPLES

CITY CAFE

COLORED ENTRANCE

Against Discrimination

Between the two world wars, in large American cities, there was a marked growth in the population of black ghettos. In the sixties these ghettos became the scene of violent race riots which often led to incidents of police brutality (left above). Having long preached against segregation (above, and left below) leaders now started a decisive struggle against racial discrimination. The struggle for social equality and respect for cultural differences grew intense. The idea of a return to Africa even met with some success (opposite).

Martin Luther King, Jr., (above, with President Lyndon B. Johnson) had a historic success in 1963, with the nonviolent March on Washington, D.C., in which 250,000 people participated. Black Muslim Malcolm X (opposite above), who favored counterviolence instead of nonviolence, was the precursor of the concept of "Black Power," spread by Stokely Carmichael and the Black Panther party (below, in a demonstration).

The Tenor Saxophone, Mouthpiece of the Black Community in Revolt

John Coltrane exerted an unequaled fascination on the young generation. His predominant instrument, the tenor saxophone, was particularly meaningful to them. In the fifties, the "howling" saxophones of rhythm and blues had reinforced the virile image of the tenor; this image allowed for the most direct expression, from the low, violent-tempered register to the exasperation expressed by the shrill.

During the period of free jazz, three other instrumentalists in particular used it for the requirements of their respective projects. Pharoah Sanders continued the work of John Coltrane, with whom he had been associated for some time. He developed an extremely mystical and incantatory approach and borrowed exotic musical forms and instruments from many non-Western musical sources. Archie Shepp turned himself into a historian of African-American music through his emotional rereadings of John Coltrane, Duke Ellington, and Charlie Parker, and soul, blues, and gospel music. Albert Ayler dared to scream. Mixing the most naive melodies for children with densely resonant fabrics, he placed conventional language beyond expression, favoring the immediacy of feeling.

Accessories and Paroxysms

One hallmark of free jazz is that it rarely left any instrument out.

Albert Ayler's strange frenzy (1970, left): generous, laden with tenderness, carrying a message of love and peace. There was no irony in his fanfare tunes, Broadway ditties, or rhythm and blues melodies. On the contrary, if he evoked them he did so to shake up and let go of the conventions and formal framework that compress their emotional power. Hence his hyperlyricism, reaching the saturation point. Ayler's whole art resided in this tragic quest for a basic, personal, melodic expression that goes beyond the codes of the common language and to which he had to nevertheless return in order not to sink into an illegibility equivalent to silence.

Many jazz musicians have played more than one instrument (notably sax players, who frequently play everything from the soprano to the baritone—and the flute as well). Free jazz systematized this phenomenon. Although he was on the fringe of "the new thing," Roland Kirk (left) transformed the playing of more than one instrument into something new. He played three saxophones at the same time, sang into his flute, and even used various whistles and sirens. Below: Saxophone player Archie Shepp.

In fact, its practitioners liked to play instruments other than the ones they specialized in. Ornette Coleman, for example, decided to begin to play the violin and trumpet—despite a most rudimentary technique. Accidental sounds (squawks, squeaks, gurgles, bumps, bangs, and so on) were integrated into the music. Drummers such as Sunny Murray decided to put the traditional notion of keeping time aside, choosing to vibrate, murmur, and rustle instead.

Blazing important trails for the future, free jazz was the answer to the concerns of a black community—and, more widely, an entire generation—in crisis. However, when the Beatles burst forth and rock music came to the fore, everything came together in a new way, relegating jazz to the periphery.

"Meditation for Integration"

"If you want to play, play a black instrument. Learn the

bass." It was on this advice that Charles Mingus gave up his vocation as a classical cellist to become one of the greatest double bass players of bop. Still, he retained a tremendous amount of bitterness from this decision—some have blamed this for the violent and unpredictable behavior that marked his numerous collaborations. Claiming the earthy realism of the blues and the spiritual that impregnated all of his work and fed his strong antiracist positions, Mingus remained preoccupied with the erudite structures he encountered while studying Béla Bartók and the romantic repertoire.

He kept his aesthetic identity crisis going while he worked with Lennie Tristano and the representatives of the third stream. In the course of the fifties, he went from being solely an instrumentalist (he played the bass) to become, as the head of his Jazz Workshop, one of the most original composers

Two historic free jazz recordings (above). The piano hardly had a place in free jazz, except under the fingers of Cecil Taylor (left).

and bandleaders since Duke Ellington.

Mingus was not fully capable of accepting all the requirements of free jazz. Still, his music proved to be very innovative: He alternated "spontaneous polyphony" with classical counterpoint and—always terribly effectively—relentlessly varied the tempo and the beat, and he solicited the most unheard-of instrumental timbres.

A formidable agitator, from 1959 on he pulled Eric Dolphy, the saxophone, clarinet, and flute player, in his wake. Without ever identifying completely with the extreme solutions of free jazz, Dolphy imposed a discontinuous melodic line, following violent breaks that somehow never escaped from his control.

Long after Dolphy's death in 1964, Charles Mingus was still mourning this visionary partner in whom he had found the ideal instrumental echo of his concerns as composer and arranger. Mingus' concerns endured, however, into the late sixties.

Free Jazz: A Second Breath

Ever since Ornette Coleman's double quartet, many experiments attempted to organize the newfound freedom of jazz or cause the power of collective improvisation— at the core of large groups— to explode. While Alan Silva worked on the

After 1955 Cecil Taylor (below) became a towering figure in free jazz. During his quasi-athletic performances, he used the piano as a percussion instrument in a resonant flow that he managed to mold according to conceptions evocative of the work of various contemporary composers.

Oh Yeah (above), a classic Charles Mingus recording, has a title that recalls the interpolations and interjections of the congregations in black churches. The famous "Fables of Faubus," censured by Columbia in 1959, is on *Mingus Ah Um* (below). Violently sarcastic, the text takes Arkansas Governor Orval Faubus to task for having opposed school integration in Little Rock in 1957. The ferocious dialogue between Mingus (left) and his drummer, Dannie Richmond, was restored under the title "Original Faubus Fables" on the album *Mingus,* issued by the Candid Company.

density of resonant layers by superimposing individual sounds, Sun Ra linked up with a tradition of exoticism and the fantastic, associated with the big bands of the thirties.

Moreover, numerous musicians came together in associations to produce and distribute their own music, which was said to be hard to sell. One of these, the Chicago-based Association for the Advancement of Creative Musicians (AACM), contributed to restarting the dynamism of free jazz just when the movement had begun to falter. Created in 1965 in Chicago by pianist Muhal Richard Abrams, the

The talent of Eric Dolphy (left): In 1961 he put together a quintet with Booker Little (trumpet), Mal Waldron (piano), and Richard Davis and Ed Blackwell (rhythm); and in 1964 he recorded *Out to Lunch* (above) with Freddie Hubbard, Bobby Hutcherson, Richard Davis, and Tony Williams.

Below: The pianist, arranger, and bandleader Sun Ra.

Opposite: Malachi Favors, the double bass player of the Art Ensemble of Chicago.

AACM pulled together a variety of figures who would be prominent in free jazz in the seventies.

While the Art Ensemble of Chicago played on light and shade and on the dramatic organization of time, Anthony Braxton, an AACM member, referred directly to Eric Dolphy but also to such white musicians as Lee Konitz and Paul Desmond and to 20th-century classical composers as well. Particularly popular during the sixties, Braxton revealed the talents of many musicians, such as the trombone virtuoso George Lewis and the pianist Anthony Davis.

The Loft Generation

During this time innumerable artists settled in the warehouses and abandoned studios of certain areas of New York City and transformed them into living quarters, spaces for work, and centers for distributing their records. In these places, the musicians were able to express themselves and produce their work without having to be concerned about the commercial aspects of the traditional clubs or disturbing their neighbors. Interdependent with the elders of free jazz, they were preoccupied with the isolation of the free movement and gladly publicized their concern about returning to a rhythmic and melodic legibility. Thus, when they listened to Albert Ayler or David Murray, they made every effort to extract the lyrical dimension of the music.

The new excitement—which corresponded to a similar feeling in all the arts—facilitated exchanges between the heirs to free jazz and bop. Nevertheless, Ornette Coleman then opened his "harmolodic" universe in an entirely different direction. His funk quartet made a direct reference to the harshness of popular black music, inherited from James Brown.

European Jazz Developed on a Different Course from the American Model

Though an American form, jazz, of course, does have practitioners outside the United States. France, especially, has embraced jazz since its earliest days; it can be said that it all began there with Django Reinhardt in the thirties. Ending France's isolation during World War II, the American troops arrived in 1944, and the first bebop records were not long in following. For more than fifteen years there was no safe haven outside of bebop or New Orleans orthodoxy. Such rare exceptions as Martial Solal or André Hodeir only proved the rule.

With the explosion of free jazz, however, everything suddenly became possible. In Europe it became fashionable to reject the criteria of "old-fashioned jazz" at the same time that "bourgeois" art was being decried.

ANTHONY BRAXTON
COMPOSITION 98

In the late sixties Anthony Braxton reconciled the acquisitions of free jazz with a real concern for structure. His scores (below), the titles of his pieces, and his album covers (above) are evidence of his work. He toured Europe in 1969 (poster opposite).

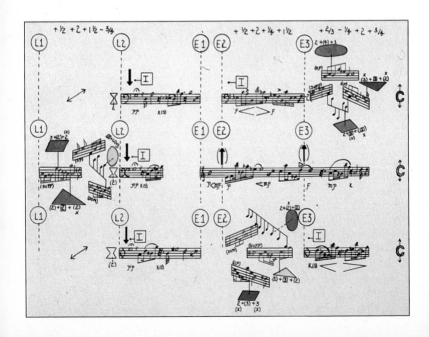

Throughout Europe, those rare big bands that were still active abandoned formal dress for blue jeans and left their platforms to mix with each other in an informal alignment that sometimes moved into a fanfare to the audience.

The roles inside the band were also called into question, and some small groups went so far as to do without a rhythm section altogether; others reduced themselves to a duo. If such changes were a response to the economic difficulties free jazz—which was not very marketable—encountered, they were also one way of experiencing

special affinities in a more intimate dramatic art. With such musicians as Mike Westbrook and Willem Breuker, these "stagings" sometimes took on true dramatic form.

The Quest for and Rejection of Memory

Two kinds of paradoxical and complementary approaches were at work in what was called

In the thirties, following the lead of American improvisers, Django Reinhardt (opposite above) was in the forefront of European jazz. Thirty years after the assimilation of bebop, European jazz gained autonomy through its contact with free jazz. In England saxophone player Evan Parker and guitarist Derek Bailey tended toward "immediate invention" and the "unpublished" (instead of the "learned" and the "already played"). In the Netherlands Willem Breuker (left and below) linked up with Germanic traditions: fanfares, Kurt Weill's influence, and Brechtian musical theater.

"European improvised music," for want of daring to call it "jazz" any longer.

For some, who turned their backs on the essence of jazz, it was a question of tracking down the phenomenon of memory in order to free themselves from it and help them move away from the rigors of the battlefield of improvisation. But whether it was to parody or magnify improvisation, many European improvisers were deeply concerned with their heritage.

If cultural references were the object of devastating derision for the Dutch drummer Han Bennink and the German saxophone player Peter Brötzmann, they called forth tender impulses from Michel Portal when he grabbed the silvery bandonion (a South American accordion) or evoked his Basque origins.

Freedom: The Power of Improvisation

Real, imaginary, or borrowed, personal folklore became one of the major concerns of the improvisers in the sixties around the world. The unbridled expression of free jazz served as an instrument for the cultural recovery of threatened identities. In Western urban societies, the inhabitants of which were deprived of deep roots, improvisation allowed for exploitation of the many musical messages transmitted by the media from the four corners of the world and from every era.

But free jazz, of course, was not the only agent of this kind of evolution. Other roads, arising from different forms of music and different cultural pressures, also opened up in the sixties.

A fter becoming known in the wake of Ornette Coleman on Don Cherry's famous *Complete Communion,* the Argentine saxophone player Gato Barbieri (below) took a decisive turn in 1968 through his contact with the South African pianist Dollar Brand. Marked by his childhood contacts with the Xhosa population (South Africa), the pianist and bandleader Chris McGregor (opposite) fled apartheid in 1964 with The Blue Notes, a multiracial sextet. In Europe he created the Brotherhood of Breath.

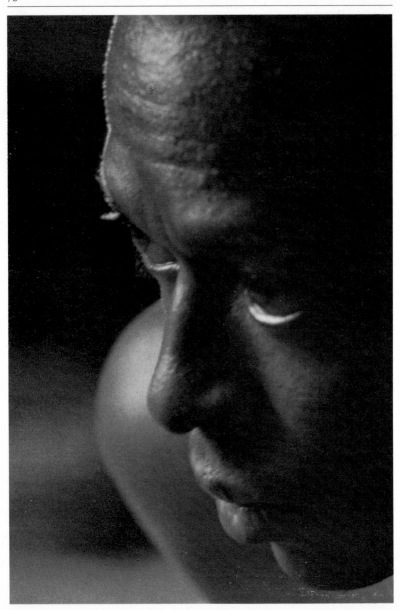

During the sixties and later, other musicians preferred to assimilate what the heralds of free jazz rejected. Far from seeing technique as an obstacle to feeling, they embraced it. Jazz widened its landscape to include influences it encountered around the world: rock, classical, and traditional forms of music.

CHAPTER IV
THE ROAD TO CHANGE

Details of two album covers: Miles Davis' *Nefertiti* (opposite) and Joe Henderson's *In 'n Out*.

In looking to the past jazz critics, historians, and theoreticians have often neglected those musicians who, coming from swing, formed separate groups on the fringes of the bop evolution (Nat King Cole, Erroll Garner) or groups even more modern than the moderns themselves (Herbie Nichols, Paul Gonsalves). Others have suffered the same neglect for having advanced at their own pace, removed from the free jazz movement (Martial Solal, Sonny Rollins), or for having simply stopped in the clearing they had found in order to explore it in relentless detail (Oscar Peterson, George Shearing).

On the Fringes of the Free

In its rush to explain history, jazz criticism has often been mistaken in presenting the explosion of free jazz and the supremacy of improvisation over writing as the sole significant developments of the sixties. After this decade the history of jazz no longer moved in one direction; many tendencies showed themselves on

One day somebody asked Duke Ellington what he thought of the avant-garde. He answered simply: "For the avant-garde I have Paul Gonsalves." Reporting this quote, sax player David Murray added: "If you want to talk about lyricism, Paul Gonsalves is it." Despite this sort of attention, Gonsalves (left) occupies only a very small place in jazz-history books.

For inspiration, saxophone players today look to once-marginal musicians such as Joe Henderson (opposite) and Jackie McLean, who performed outside the mainstream of free jazz in the sixties. In this way, they avoided the ubiquitous influence exercised by Michael Brecker and David Sanborn.

the fringes of free jazz. Besides Charles Mingus and Eric Dolphy, others, influenced by Horace Silver, John Coltrane, Miles Davis, and Ornette Coleman (some recording under the Blue Note and Candid labels), declared themselves outside of any identifiable group. Musical language advanced, feeding both the autonomy of the improviser and the emancipation of rhythm. The players of "the new thing," involved in a political struggle, embraced their cultural heritage, but, in contrast, a large number of their contemporaries demanded the freedom to control, master, and assimilate what they wanted from the cultural environment at large, from classical music to free jazz.

A "Barroom Piano Player"

This is how Bill Evans was appraised when free jazz exploded. Later, the critics realized that circumspectly, and without being the leader of any particular

Born in 1929, the young Bill Evans (opposite, below left) first studied the violin. He later shifted to the piano, which he studied in New Orleans, and by 1954 he was a master of harmony and composition. In 1956 Evans recorded *New Jazz Conceptions,* followed by *Everybody Digs Bill Evans.* His trio career had its first success with the 1961 live recordings from the Village Vanguard in New York. He also led small groups, as on *Interplay* (1962).

current, he had led as profound a revolution as John Coltrane or Ornette Coleman. Without ever systematizing the contributions of modal jazz (which he helped found), he drew deep inspiration from it. His work as a composer surely borrowed from the charms of the old standards, of which he was very fond; but he lightened their often-limited harmonic frames and broadened the field of melodic possibilities.

More significantly, due to the quality of his touch, he inaugurated a new approach to the jazz piano, which, until that point, had primarily been used as a percussion instrument. Bill Evans was not a barroom piano player; he was a concert pianist. His trio (piano, double bass, drums), which he used as a chamber orchestra, broke new ground.

From 1960 to 1961, Scott LaFaro (bass) and Paul Motian (drums) freed themselves from their role as mere accompanists and became soloists on an equal footing with the piano; the three participated in a triangular conversation. Collective and interactive, improvisation became more than ever a question of mutual listening and finding one's own place while treating the others' with respect. The revolution led by John Coltrane with sound and fury was conducted by Bill Evans' trios with great delicacy that evoked the intimacy of Claude Debussy.

The years 1965–8 were a time of intense creativity for Miles Davis, evidenced by the albums *E.S.P.* (1965), *Sorcerer* (1967), and *Filles de Kilimanjaro* (1968). His successive wives—dancer Frances Taylor, actress Cicely Tyson, and singer Betty Mabry—are shown on these album covers.

Thus, along with such contemporaries as Jim Hall, who shared his concerns, Bill Evans left his mark on generations of musicians: on pianists, of course (Keith Jarrett, Paul Bley, and Chick Corea), but also on drummers (Jack DeJohnette), bass players (Gary Peacock), guitarists (Pat Metheny), vibraphonists (Gary Burton), and saxophone players, trumpet players, and bandleaders.

The Endurance of Miles Davis

Throughout the sixties Miles Davis was haunted by the short time (1958–9) Bill Evans and John Coltrane were both in his group. Twice he replaced his pianist, first with Wynton Kelly, then with Herbie Hancock, who combined the refinements of Bill Evans and the more vigorous statements of the funk pianists. On the other hand, it took him several years before he found the replacement for John Coltrane in the person of Wayne Shorter.

When he did, a new era opened up for Miles Davis, marked by recordings that today are considered to be masterpieces of modern jazz for small groups. Thus, from one year to the next, *E.S.P.*, *Miles Smiles*, *Nefertiti*, and *Miles in the Sky*, among others, raised and then answered a series of musical questions. Davis' quintet was, at that time, a truly experimental group—each entrance into the studio would bring a new development.

In its way, the rhythm section exploited the heritage of the Bill Evans trio: Herbie Hancock (piano) was suggestive; Ron Carter (bass) no longer stated the tempo systematically but imposed a powerful sense of pulsation; Tony

Williams (drums), sophisticated and daring, freed himself from the accompanist's role. He took the Elvin Jones' polyrhythm, gave it air, and diversified it by superimposing figures conceived in binary measures. In session after session, the quintet explored a repertoire dependent on Wayne Shorter's innovative ideas. Shorter, a master improviser, showed Davis a way to widen the range of liberties allowed by modal playing even further. On the stage Davis stayed with a more conventional program, but the risks he took in the studio changed the way the public saw the band.

Like the innovations of Charlie Parker twenty years earlier, these measures, ground-breaking at the time, have become the conventions of small-group jazz.

The Beatles (above) had a tremendous influence on the music of the sixties—rock, obviously, but jazz as well—with their new way of conceiving the group and producing records.

The Rock Explosion

At the end of the sixties, strengthened by his quintet's experiments, Miles Davis was ripe for bringing himself before rock and its immense audience.

A fusion of country music and black rock and roll (derived from boogie), rock was created by white artists in the mid-fifties. Over the next decade, it adopted the effective rhythm sections of rhythm and blues and profited by carrying soul and other types of American music forward. At the same time it received support from new recording and production methods and made use of the electric instruments that had appeared with the urban blues.

Instrumental performances became increasingly important not only with rock—leading to the appearance of "guitar heroes"—but also with the transformation of musical forms. In the late sixties, "rockers" invaded realms hitherto reserved for better-informed kinds of music, such as classical, jazz, and certain types of traditional non-European music. After this point rock could be played for extended periods, and huge sound systems were installed, making enormous outdoor concerts possible.

The huge outdoor musical gatherings that blossomed after Woodstock benefited the jazz musicians who invented jazz-rock.

The Hippie Era

In England, the line between jazz and rock was a thin one: Both forms verged close to rhythm and blues as well as the blues revival. Various future jazz players and rock stars all received their training in Alexis Korner's or Graham Bond's groups. "Progressive rock" and avant-garde jazz ran on parallel tracks at the end of the decade, and such groups as Soft Machine left a mark on entire generations of musicians and listeners. In the United States white rock groups such as Blood, Sweat and Tears and Chicago featured rhythm-and-blues brass sections.

Many jazz musicians were concerned about the rise of rock. Charles Lloyd, accompanied by Keith Jarrett, for one, was successful in adapting a Coltranian

With the help of Jimi Hendrix (above) and Sly Stone (below) Miles Davis developed new sounds and a new rhythmic style.

feeling to the melodic ingenuity of the "folk revival" and Beatles songs—all against the background of a light show. With Cannonball Adderley, in a context oriented more toward the black roots of rhythm and blues, others experimented with the electric piano invented by Harold Rhodes and Leo Fender.

Miles Plugged In His Trumpet

By now fed up with the elitism of free jazz and with rock (which, he said, diverted and weakened rhythm and blues), Miles Davis turned his full attention to popular black music, and particularly to the funk of Sly and the Family Stone. Sly Stone practiced a violent and direct aesthetic inherited from James Brown.

In 1968 Miles met Jimi Hendrix, the hero of rock guitar. Hendrix knew how to funnel the force of blues to the universe of pop. Hearing him, Miles Davis understood that the guitar, on the margin until then, was destined to be in the forefront of the evolution of jazz. Indeed, at that point keyboards, bass, and even wind instruments were following in the guitar's footsteps, becoming electrified. The volume increased, and new types of sound appeared. After 1969, when Miles recorded *In a Silent Way* with John McLaughlin, a young guitarist from the English stage, electronics were a standard part of his world.

Limiting his written work to a few suggestive measures, hooking his trumpet up to a wa-wa pedal, Miles set off true electronic revels on the records that followed. On them, there was a new combination of electric guitar, bass guitar, various keyboards, percussion instruments from the world over, and the binary hammering inherited from Tony Williams.

The Jazz-Rock of Miles Davis' Children

Innumerable musicians who were temporarily part of Davis' band attempted to prolong that musical experience and hold on to the public won through that contact. Transposing the energy of rock into their

*B*itches Brew, recorded by Miles Davis in August 1969, confirmed the turn he had taken a few months earlier with *In a Silent Way.* After this point he played long suites for hours on end; they had to be edited in order to fit onto records. He conquered the audiences at the huge festivals, where he appeared on the same stage as rock stars (whose limited technique Davis considered with definite disdain). A growing number of white jazz musicians were affected by this music. Thus, from the mid-sixties on, Gary Burton and his double bass player, Steve Swallow, went back to their country roots and reinterpreted Bob Dylan's early folk rock. The guitar player Larry Coryell explored the effects of saturation and feedback the rock musicians could obtain with their powerful amplifiers.

By opening up to jazz-rock, jazz festivals changed their look (opposite). Electronic equipment moved onto the stage, and drum sections were expanded in order to respond to the ever-more-spectacular performances, both in terms of instrumental technique and stage presence. Herbie Hancock is at left, and Alphonse Mouzon is below.

bands, they put their savoir faire as jazz musicians to the service of jazz-rock. John McLaughlin, for example, met with great success with his Mahavishnu Orchestra, starting in 1971. He allied a virtuosic writing and the incantations inherited from John Coltrane to a concern with technical performance that excited the rock audience. Mystical, like Coltrane, and fascinated with India, he blended the metric and modal sophistication of Indian music with the rhythmic and harmonic effectiveness of rhythm and blues.

The pianist Jan Hammer was a pioneer in exploring the phrasing possibilities offered by the first electronic keyboards. The violinist Jerry Goodman attracted the public's attention, and the drummer Billy Cobham gave proof of fascinating technique in music with uneven meters.

Through their power, speed of execution, and impressive equipment, the

drummers unleashed great excitement.
Now in the forefront of their bands, leaders such as
Tony Williams or Billy Cobham often eclipsed the
fame of their entourage.

This, however, was not the case with Lenny White
(drums) and Stanley Clarke (the first great electric
bass soloist), who played with Chick Corea's group,
Return to Forever. As for Corea himself, who had
shared in Miles Davis' first electronic experiments, his
keyboard virtuosity and brilliant writing were
seductive. Swinging toward the Spanish with the
addition of the guitarist Al DiMeola, the strong Latin
feeling in his repertoire delighted the public.

Also emerging from Miles Davis' universe, Herbie
Hancock created a group that was more profoundly
anchored in the popular African-American tradition.
Leaning on the deep-sounding "drop" of the
drummer Harvey Mason, Hancock's music became
funkier than Davis'. More accessible to the general
public, it was enormously successful, particularly with

Weather Report
spent a long time
looking for rhythm as
effective in the binary as
in the ternary realm; the
drummer's performances
became especially
exhausting. It even
became necessary to have
two drummers along on
their tours. The group
probably entered a
rhythmic state of grace
with the arrival of the
big-band drummer Peter
Erskine and electric bass
player Jaco Pastorius
(above right; above left,
the saxophone player and
composer Wayne
Shorter). Pastorius, with
his remarkable stage
presence, created a furor
at the time.

the album that takes its title from the name of the group: *Head Hunters.* Like Chick Corea, who was now swinging between acoustic and electronic music, Hancock alternated successful inroads into "electro-funk" with returns to formulas close to the spirit of the Miles Davis quintet of the sixties.

Weather Report

Again, it was former members of Miles Davis' groups who constituted the core of the most enduring group of this type: Weather Report. In late 1970 Wayne Shorter, Joe Zawinul (piano), and Miroslav Vitous (bass) invited Alphonse Mouzon (drums) and Airto Moreira (exotic percussion instruments) to create climates of a most meteorological diversity. Their repertoire was often put together like classical program music—it told a story in the same way symphonic poems composed by European musicians of the 19th century did. Weather Report's music was

With its fourth record, *Mysterious Traveler* (1973), Weather Report conquered the general public and obtained full support from Columbia Records at the same time. Its commercial ambitions continued to be obvious through *Black Market* (1976), on which the influence of African and Brazilian music reached its peak. It is on the following album, *Heavy Weather,* that the famous title "Birdland" can be found. *Night Passage,* in 1980, represented the pinnacle of achievement for the Pastorius/Erskine tandem. Carried by a new rhythm section (Victor Bailey, Omar Hakim), their next-to-last album, *Sportin' Life,* was a masterpiece of the digital technology of the eighties.

then directed toward an ever-more-diverse fusion of influences, in which the binary scanning of rock and Latin music became more and more important. In 1974 Vitous made way for the electric bass player Alphonso Johnson, while Joe Zawinul began to explore the power of synthesizers. But the group did not receive the blessing of the public until the 1976 arrival of Jaco Pastorius, who, until his death in 1987, was the most original virtuoso of the electric bass. The records *Black Market* (1976) and *Heavy Weather* (1977) are counted among the finest successes of the genre. On this last album, the title "Birdland," which paid homage to the tradition of the big-band entertainment of the thirties, was an overwhelming success.

Nevertheless, despite the loyalty of a vast audience and the excellent rhythm tandem of Pastorius and the drummer Peter Erskine, disagreements between Shorter and Zawinul provoked Weather Report's breakup in 1985, a decade and a half after its creation.

Fusion in the Studio

Little by little, the taste for musical crossbreeding gained acceptance. The term "fusion" was given preference over that of jazz-rock, which was considered too restrictive.

For a long time, Michael and Randy Brecker (below) were associated with group experiments: First with Dreams, with John Abercrombie and Billy Cobham, then the Brecker Brothers. A 1979 jam session at their club, Seventh Avenue South, was the beginning of the group Steps Ahead. This group featured vibraphonist Mike Mainieri, pianist Don Grolnick, Eddie Gomez on double bass, and drummer Steve Gadd. In 1987, after participating in hundreds of recordings, Michael finally recorded under his name, while Randy formed his own quintet.

Alto player David Sanborn (opposite) belongs to the same generation. Indeed, he performed with the Brecker Brothers in 1975, before forming his own groups, in which he continued to collaborate with the most representative fusion musicians, such as guitar players John Scofield, Mike Stern, and Hiram Bullock.

The Brecker Brothers caused a furor. Strengthened by their experience with John Abercrombie and Billy Cobham in the group Dreams, they were able to adapt to any context what they inherited from Coltrane, juggling ternary and binary phrasing with complete ease. Randy, the trumpet player, and Michael, on sax, became unavoidable reference points for future instrumentalists, as much for their contribution to studio work as for their improvisations. The alto player David Sanborn, equally sought after by the studios, practiced a fusion just as joyful, bearing at the same time both the mark of his closeness with Stevie Wonder and the imprint of Gil Evans' band, in which he spent some time.

A Certain Need for Space

Jazz-rock continued to satisfy the youthful public well into the eighties, despite the fact that the admirers, the press, and even the musicians wearied of it. At the end of the seventies, John McLaughlin and several others returned to the virtues of the acoustic guitar. Instrumental stereotypes and the somewhat vain virtuosity of jazz-rock guitar players were specifically called into question. The reaction came from the musicians themselves. An airier tone, a more limpid melody, a lighter orchestral context—these qualities were sought after as musicians listened to their elders: Wes Montgomery, Jim Hall, and Bill Evans.

But they wanted to mix their own culture—pop songs and country music—in with this. Guitar players John Abercrombie and Pat Metheny found the space their aspirations required at the record label ECM.

ECM Aesthetics

"Editions of Contemporary Music": the identity crisis of jazz at the time was captured in the very name of this label, which didn't even dare to name the music it presented. German Manfred Eicher, a former bassist, established ECM in 1969. He was first noticed for seeking to capture

After having played in the hubbub of jazz clubs, Keith Jarrett (below) insisted on silence around him: He epitomizes the jazz musician who has become a concert artist. The popular success of his *Köln Concert* (1975) proved the popularity of the solo piano, which also benefited Chick Corea, Herbie Hancock, and Paul Bley.

a sound reminiscent of the acoustics of a concert hall rather than that of a smoky club. The technical enhancements ECM employed—precision of the stereo sound and reconstitution of the echo, and the crystal-clear rendering of instruments such as the piano, the vibraphone, and the electric and acoustic guitars—displeased old discophiles but responded to what a young public concerned with a certain ease in listening (even at the expense of authenticity) was waiting for.

Later generations, disappointed by the crumbling of revolutionary ideologies and the exhaustion of

In the seventies Keith Jarrett led two quartets, one American (Dewey Redman, Charlie Haden, Paul Motian), and one European (Jan Garbarek, Palle Danielsson, Jon Christensen)—complementary facets of a music influenced by Bach, Scott Joplin, Bud Powell, Bill Evans, Ornette Coleman, and the pop song.

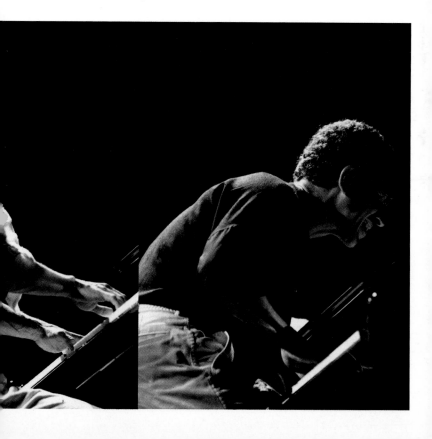

the avant-garde, have focused on defending the environment and reviving the classics. ECM and the innumerable labels that fell in step with it suggested a new "ecology" of recording and concert giving. The return to the acoustic piano was magnified by the solo formula, until that point still fairly exceptional in modern jazz. Solos by Keith Jarrett or Paul Bley and duets by Chick Corea with Herbie Hancock or Gary Burton publicized jazz as chamber music. The jazz musician now became a concert artist, and jazz concerts benefited by being listened to as seriously as recitals of classical music.

Gateway by John Abercrombie (1975, below) broke with the influence of John McLaughlin's jazz-rock. The accumulation of virtuoso phrases made a place for a lighter conception of forms, articulation, and tone. ECM helped many artists satisfy their need for space.

Using echo chambers and rerecording, John Surman (opposite above, in a "chamber music" atmosphere typical of ECM) made music inspired by the Celtic tradition.

The saxophone player Jan Garbarek (opposite below) enveloped his poignant tone in a halo of reverberation, heartily vilified by the critics. He contributed to the renewal of the saxophone by employing it in his completely personal imaginary folklore.

E vocative of northern European spaces—of a certain quality of light and air in that region—ECM album covers reflect a "new ecology of catching sound."

The State of Jazz at the End of the Seventies

In the seventies, jazz entered a neoclassical phase. From Archie Shepp to Martial Solal, the rereading of yesterday's repertoire became common practice. At the same time, with Lee Konitz, Dexter Gordon, or Art Pepper, a young public rediscovered the figures of free jazz. Increasingly numerous references to classical music drew from a wide range of sources.

Generally speaking, in the United States as in the rest of the world, young musicians claimed an encyclopedic culture in which classical, rock, and world music went side by side. From jazz, musicians retained an impressive ability to absorb and appropriate outside elements.

B orn at the start of the century, jazz must now take stock. Are its newest incarnations indications of an art running out of breath or the sign of an expanding tradition? Those who ask this question ignore the fact that, around the world, different types of music outside the mainstream have been inspired by jazz: They constitute a fanfare for the century that is nearing its end.

CHAPTER V
JAZZ BURSTS INTO PIECES

The radiant figure of Gil Evans (left, in 1987, just before his death) leaves one hoping that jazz has a future other than the commercial. Right: An advertisement for Yves Saint-Laurent's Jazz perfume.

D iscovered playing with Art Blakey in 1980, the young Wynton Marsalis seems to have stolen Clifford Brown's virtuosity. Blind imitation, cloning, shallow technical feats? The trumpet player made his mark with an authentic remaking of hard bop, which had also influenced Miles Davis in the sixties. By degrees he went back to his New Orleans roots (see the album above, *The Majesty of the Blues*). His brother Branford (left, with Wynton) is also famous now.

In some circles, the thirties are hot and jazz is fashionable. Its look is evoked in fashion design and black-and-white advertising photographs. Its imagery pervades the movies, as the film industry exploits the stereotype of the jazz genius. Its impact is felt in rock and roll. In other words, the image and the legend of jazz still have power, even while today's improvised music tends to detach itself from it.

Historic Reissues Took Over the Recording Market

Now a well-recognized and thoroughly accepted form of music, jazz occupies a solid space on music lovers' shelves, side by side with the classics.

After 1983—which was, significantly, the year the compact disk was introduced—record companies suddenly had the opportunity to reissue and anthologize the recorded heritage of jazz at a lower cost than ever before. Even with so much focus on looking back, however, in the eighties there were still some new developments, largely restricted to neo-bop and commercial productions.

The Coming of Neo-bop

With the brothers Branford and Wynton Marsalis as its stars, neo-bop was the field developed by an elite group of young musicians trained in the school of Art Blakey's Jazz Messengers. Heirs to hard bop, on which they put a new turn after listening to the music of the Miles Davis quintet of the sixties, these young musicians were regularly accused of being nothing but copies of earlier models.

After six years of retirement, Miles Davis returned to the stage in 1981, no longer merely a great trumpet player, but one of the most elegant men in the world, the symbol of a fashionable jazz. He listened to the hits on the pop charts (Toto, Cameo) and borrowed their music (Cyndi Lauper, Scritti Politi). With *Tutu* (1987) he left Columbia for Warner, seeking the effectiveness of its recent funk releases. He went even further in this direction in 1991 (the year of his death) with his adoption of themes by Prince and his work with Flavor Flav, the rapper with Public Enemy.

Black jazz changed its face in the eighties. Women were now no longer merely singers (left, Geri Allen). Teaching, whose role has always been much underrated, became important, and young musicians turned back to their roots.

Their astoundingly advanced technique and flawless performances deprived them, said some critics, of that element of risk that made their predecessors interesting.

These not-very-subtle observations ignored the importance of the traditional element in black American music. On top of that, one must remember that despite its lightning-fast evolution in just a few decades, jazz has always counted more followers than innovators.

The adoration for the "small masters" who personalized Charlie Parker's message during the fifties is not so far removed from the admiration that the New York neo-boppers aroused thirty years later.

From the Church to the Street

African-American jazz has always sought to maintain its footing in the sociological reality from which it was born.

Such was the significance of Quincy Jones' *Back on the Block*, which came out in 1990. Taking stock of this century as it nears its end, Jones—Count Basie's former arranger and Michael Jackson's producer at the time—assembled a few of the great names of black American music, from Ray Charles to Miles Davis, along with Ella Fitzgerald and Dizzy Gillespie.

Soul music and rap welcomed jazz, as if to remind it they grew up together in black churches and on the street. From the

delicate neo-classical touch of the pianist Geri Allen to the fanfares of Lester Bowie (the Art Ensemble of Chicago's trumpet player), along with the saxophonists Kenny Garrett (like Geri Allen, trained in Detroit with the trumpet player Marcus Belgrave) or Gary Thomas

Is the sound of the white saxophonists who are heirs to Michael Brecker too clean? Should one instead blame a certain type of production, too concerned with technical perfection and therefore generating a certain coldness? David Liebman (below) has escaped such criticisms because of his originality and his musical generosity.

(discovered while with Jack DeJohnette and Miles Davis)—the same concern with roots, the same attention to the latest developments of funk, and an openness of spirit that confirmed the choices musicians made in the sixties were found everywhere.

What do the following have in common: Wynton Marsalis in his three-piece suit, the rap group 2 Live Crew with its obscenities, and the jazz that came forth in the sixties, mixing the acquisitions of free jazz with the certainties of bop?

All belong to that same community—they were different reactions to the mounting economic difficulties, the marginalization of the most disenfranchised, and the increase in the minority population in the eighties.

Jazz in Joint Ownership

The different forms of improvised music—still conveniently collected under the label of jazz—were not, of course, the exclusive property of black musicians at this time. Numerous white musicians also appropriated the heritage of jazz: David Liebman and Richard Beirach, more than anyone else, continued to deepen the heritage of John

Big bands aren't what they used to be: Since Gil Evans, the French horn and tuba have been integrated into the brass section, the woodwind section has been expanded (double reeds and flutes enriching the palette of the saxophones and clarinets), the number of percussion instruments has increased, the guitar (which disappeared in the forties) has returned, and synthesizers have been adopted. Composition has become more flexible and mobile, sometimes even impudent, as can be seen in the work of Carla Bley (above).

Coltrane and Bill Evans; Keith Jarrett gave new life to old standards and to the traditional rhythm section in the vein of Bill Evans; Pat Metheny fed his superproductions, tinged with pop, Brazilian, and country music, with inspirations from Ornette Coleman and Wes Montgomery.

Black producers, from Quincy Jones to Marcus Miller, have had an undeniable impact in the last decade. But another force since the sixties has been the white jazz musicians who have changed the direction of the sound as well, thanks to personalities such as Michael

A true pop star, navigating between the sublime and the facile, Pat Metheny (above) continues to claim the heritage of Ornette Coleman, Jim Hall, and Wes Montgomery. With John Abercrombie, John Scofield, and Bill Frisell, he has put a vitality back into the jazz guitar. Left: The Vienna Art Orchestra, an institution of European jazz.

Brecker, David Sanborn, and the guitarist
Larry Carlton. One always hears their names
in this regard.

Studio work has allowed jazz-rock to
become open to a variety of other influences.
Jazz has profited commercially from such
borrowings.

With Latin music all the rage, a new
"fusion"—evocative of sun and health—
was able to respond to the demand of a
public fond of tonic music as well as to a
youthful audience concerned with making
the most of the positive aspects of its
racial diversity.

A bove: Hermeto
Pascoal, a folkloric
and visionary figure from
northeastern Brazil, knew
how to bring together the
most diverse resonant
echoes into one music.

The Reawakening of Big Bands

Since the forties, big bands were increasingly
the domain of white musicians. In the course of
the sixties, Don Ellis outdistanced the metric
preoccupations of jazz-rock. Carla Bley, with her
compositions evoking the worlds of Charles Ives, Erik
Satie, and Kurt Weill, introduced a dimension
of parody.

As for Gil Evans and George Russell, their
invariably avant-garde writing led them to the
dismantling of the structures of the big band,
frequently shrinking the wind section, shifting
the weight to the rhythm section, and adopting a
freedom inherited from free jazz. *Aura* (1989) was
the first record Miles Davis brought out with a
large group since he recorded *Quiet Nights* with Gil
Evans in 1962.

Jazz for All

In the past the jazz community could be depicted as
one big family divided by domestic conflict, but by
the end of the eighties that family seemed to be
dissolving. If contemporary jazz musicians still return
to the standards as an obligatory exercise in style or as
the opportunity to express their devotion to tradition,

the repertoire and practices are no longer homogeneous enough to allow an encounter between musicians of different generations.

And jazz fans? Feeling rather lost, the lovers of early jazz see no great connection between all this and the colorful legend of New Orleans that brought them to the field in the first place. Then there are other specialists: collectors of West Coast music and those fondly reminiscent of the radical sixties and seventies. All three share a protest against ECM productions, which they consider sterile and devoid of swing.

The New Sounds of Jazz

While the fans attached to their collections of 78s—who rebel against the compact disk—

When the French government created the Orchestre National de Jazz (ONJ), it provoked a dispute: How could an improvisational art, an art of cultural resistance, be placed under the aegis of the state? Thanks to its conductors, including François Jeanneau (below, with the group in 1986), the ONJ managed to command attention in the landscape of French jazz.

remain an extreme case, it *is* true that the sound of jazz and the nature of the studio work have changed considerably. In the past, recordings were made in one or several takes, from which the best one would be chosen. Today, multitrack tape recorders allow the most satisfying fragments from distinct takes to be edited together. Frequently, especially with electric fusion groups, the instrumentalists are recorded one after the other and a piece is put together without any of the different musicians even meeting in the studio. For all, including acoustic musicians, corrective work is done on the different tracks, for various reasons, even to arrive again at the artistic content of the work.

These operations have evolved considerably with the appearance of digital technology, which permits the sound to be manipulated by computers. Synthesizers, too, have benefited from this. New electronic devices abound: various keyboards, sequencers, rhythm boxes, and electronic wind instruments—not to mention the "sampler," which permits electronic verification of the characteristics of a sound in order to either reproduce it just as it is or to deform it.

Insects and Pygmies

With the use of technology, insect sounds and Pygmy choirs have been pirated and injected into recordings. One would be tempted to say that through these high-tech means jazz is rediscovering cultural appropriation— its first function.

Indeed, by the end of the eighties there was more appropriation than ever before, in both acoustic and electric jazz. Jazz musicians have picked up and assimilated everything that has presented itself. This is what one might call a real fusion music.

Tony Hymans featured native Americans on his album *Oyaté* (opposite), an homage to the great chiefs.

Below: Michael Brecker.

These pretexts and the standards and conventions of classical jazz are no longer required. A much larger heritage—classical music, urban and rural traditions, academic music and music of the streets, rock and country, free jazz, and various other sounds—is being looked at, borrowed from, and generally shaken up.

A Power Intact

Did jazz die in the eighties? Maybe it died years

earlier, with Ornette Coleman, Gil Evans, Charlie Parker, or even, simply, the minute it left New Orleans. All this is surely debatable. But the only fact that matters is this: The explosion of black American music at the beginning of the century has turned the history of music upside down.

The immense musical river that set off from New Orleans has spawned numerous tributaries and today has arrived at its delta. Some of its large streams have gotten lost. In this decompartmentalized, cosmopolitan, and multicolored space, the standard-bearers of jazz have disappeared. They have left room for a permissiveness and a wild variety of individual styles, all carried by the impulse that was called swing in the thirties, which, in diversifying, has lost none of its power.

The Indian percussionist Trilok Gurtu (opposite above), the French organist Eddy Louiss (left) and his Multicolor Feeling, Bill Frisell, Jerry Gonzalez, Sixun (covers above), and Nana Vasconcelos (overleaf): The diversity of contemporary jazz.

Of Russian and Irish descent, Kip Hanrahan (opposite below) brought together representatives of different communities in the Bronx in musical groups as strange as they were temporary.

DOCUMENTS

The Turning Point

At the end of the forties, jazz changed its look. Dizzy Gillespie prepared the way for the fusion of jazz and Latin rhythms. Musicians gathered in Gil Evans' room asked each other a thousand questions, and from their answers grew a new musical concept, allowing Miles Davis to free himself from the "old tricks" of bop.

Gil Evans' Room

George Russell, Miles Davis, and Gil Evans remember.

In 1948, a visitor would come down a staircase on West 55th Street in Manhattan to the basement of a gray brick building and, after having knocked out of mere courtesy, would come in the always open door of the world of Gil Evans. In a barely lighted room, a record player was continuously playing Alban Berg, Ravel, Lester Young, Ellington, or an occasional resident: Charlie Parker. There were hundreds of records, books by Hermann Hesse, poems by Dylan Thomas and e. e. cummings, abstract paintings left by one of the guests passing through, and a cat named Becky.

New York was ablaze with creative

Gil Evans.

energy. Thelonious Monk was being innovative with his brilliant music at the Downbeat Club where Billie Holiday often shared billing with him. Morton Feldman, John Cage, LaMonte Young, Stephan Wolpe, and Gunther Schuller were breaking new ground before a large and enthusiastic audience. Pollock, Kline, and Calder were exploring the visual arts. The Open Theater was breaking down traditionalism in the theater. On Broadway, Brando, Clift, and Dean were changing the common ideas about acting by practicing Strasberg's "Method." Charlie Parker was changing the aesthetics of American music every evening at the Three Deuces. His revolutionary impact on music has been compared to that of Dylan Thomas on the English language.

During this extraordinary cultural period, Gil Evans' room became a refuge for seekers and he our guru. I don't think that he ever refused a musician who had a problem. He had the gift of taking the error upon himself, and of breathing energy into someone in order to look for the impossible. He was of great support to Charlie Parker, Miles Davis, and most certainly to me.

George Russell,
on the occasion of Gil Evans being granted a Doctor Honoris Causa degree,
New England Conservatory,
19 May 1985

During this time I was going over to Gil Evans' a lot, listening to what he was saying about the music. Gil and I had hit it off right away. I could relate to his musical ideas and he could relate to mine. With Gil, the question of race never entered; it was always

Miles Davis and Dizzy Gillespie.

about music. He didn't care what color you were. He was one of the first white people I had met that was like this. He was Canadian and maybe that had something to do with how he thought.

Out of *Birth of the Cool* me and Gil got to be real great friends. Gil was just the kind of guy you love being around, because he would see things nobody else saw. He loved paintings and he would show me things that I wouldn't have ever seen. Or, he would listen to an orchestration and say, "Miles, listen to the cello right here. How else do you think that he could have played that passage?" He'd make you think about s—— all the time. He used to just go inside of music and pull things out another person wouldn't normally have heard. Later he would call me up at three AM and tell me, "If you're ever depressed, Miles, just listen to 'Springsville'" (which was a great tune we put on the *Miles Ahead* album). And then he'd hang up the phone. Gil was a thinker and I loved that about him right away.

When I first met him, he used to come to listen to Bird when I was in the band. He'd come in with a whole bag of "horseradishes"—that's what we used to call radishes—that he'd be eating with salt. Here was this tall, thin, white guy from Canada who was hipper than hip. I mean, I didn't know *any* white people like him. I was used to black folks back in East St. Louis walking into places with a bag full of barbecued pig snout sandwiches and taking them out and eating them right there, right in a movie or club or anywhere. But bringing "horseradishes" to nightclubs and eating them out of a bag with salt, and a white boy? Here was Gil on East 52nd Street with all these super hip black musicians wearing peg legs and zoot suits, and here he was dressed in a cap. Man, he was something else.

Gil's basement apartment over on 55th Street was where a lot of musicians hung out. Gil's place was so dark you didn't know whether it was night or day. Max, Diz, Bird, Gerry Mulligan, George Russell, Blossom Dearie, John Lewis, Lee Konitz, and Johnny Carisi used to be at Gil's all the time. Gil had this big bed that took up a lot of space and this weird m—— cat who was always getting into everything. We would always be sitting around talking about music, or arguing about something.… But Gil was like a mother hen to all of us. He cooled everything out because he was so cool. He was a beautiful person who just

loved to be around musicians. And we loved being around him because he taught us so much, about caring for people and about music, especially arranging music.

Miles Davis
Miles, the Autobiography
1989

I was always interested in other musicians.… I was hungry for musical companionship, because I hadn't had much of it before. Like bull sessions in musical theory. Since I hadn't gone to school, I hadn't had that before.

Gil Evans
quoted in Jack Chambers
Milestones One
1983

Miles Davis' Nine-Piece Band

Miles Davis and the producer Bob Weinstock speak of the genesis of Birth of the Cool.

Gil and I had already started doing things together and everything was going real well for us. I was looking for a vehicle where I could solo more in the style that I was hearing. My music was a little slower and not so intense as Bird's. My conversations with Gil about experimenting with more subtle voicing and s—— were exciting to me. Gerry Mulligan, Gil, and I started talking about forming this group. We thought nine pieces would be the right amount of musicians to be in the band. Gil and Gerry had decided what the instruments in the band would be before I really came into the discussions. But the theory, the musical interpretation and what the band would play, was my idea.

Miles Davis.

I hired the rehearsal halls, called the rehearsals, and got things done. I was doing this s—— with Gil and Gerry on the side from the summer of 1948 until we recorded in January and April of 1949 and then again in March 1950. I got us some jobs and made the contact at Capitol Records to do the recording. But working with Gil really got me into writing compositions. I would play them for Gil on the piano at his apartment.

I remember when we started to get the nonet together that I wanted Sonny Stitt on alto saxophone. Sonny sounded a lot like Bird, so I thought of him right away. But Gerry Mulligan wanted Lee Konitz because he had a light sound rather than a hard bebop sound. He felt that this kind of sound was what was going to make the album and the band different. Gerry felt that with me, Al McKibbon, Max Roach, and John Lewis all in the group and all coming from bebop, it might just be the same old thing all over again, so I took his advice and hired Lee Konitz....

A lot of people thought the s—— we were playing was strange. I remember

Tal Farlow, Novosel, and Red Norvo.

Barry Ulanov of *Metronome* magazine being a little confused about the music we played. Count Basie used to listen every night that we were there opposite him, and he liked it. He told me that it was "slow and strange, but good, real good." A lot of the other musicians who used to come hear the band liked it also, including Bird. But Pete Rugolo of Capitol Records really liked what he heard and he asked me if he could record us for Capitol....

Birth of the Cool came from black musical roots. It came from Duke Ellington. We were trying to sound like Claude Thornhill, but he had gotten his s—— from Duke Ellington and Fletcher Henderson. Gil Evans himself was a big fan of Duke's and Billy Strayhorn's, and Gil was the arranger for *Birth of the Cool.*

Miles Davis
Miles, the Autobiography

Gil Evans had a tremendous influence on Miles' musical thinking.... He kept telling me, "Get Gil Evans, get him to do an album. He's beautiful." I think that Miles found his true element there, at *that* time. Here was a chance for all his sensitivity, compared to Bird's savageness and deep fire and emotion, which was overpowering Miles every time they played on the same stand; here was an outlet for Miles Davis to let out the sensitivity that he had....

Bob Weinstock
Chambers, *Milestones One*

The Lighthouse Café

The bassist Howard Rumsey, leader of the Lighthouse All Stars, remembers the beginnings of West Coast cool.

Howard Rumsey: I knew Hermosa Beach.... The Lighthouse was the only place with a stage. I went to find John Levine to suggest that he organize jam sessions on Sunday afternoons.... He couldn't handle it. So I said to him: "You're not working anyway, so what have you got to lose?"

"Don't you know that Sunday is the worst day for selling drinks?"

"Let's try it, anyway!" I found some guys who could play loudly, we sat down in front of the door the following Sunday, and within one hour there were more people than there had been in a week.

Shorty Rogers: We were free on Mondays and Tuesdays, but on Sundays we played from two in the afternoon until two in the morning. Physically it was very hard, but we were young and the place was terrific. The drinks weren't expensive, there was no cover charge.... It was always crowded. Since the ocean was only a few yards away, there would often be a listener in a bathing suit when we opened. And sometimes the same person in a bathing suit was still there at two in the morning.

The Lighthouse was also a kind of laboratory for the young musicians you were then?

I think so, especially for Jimmy and me, who were constantly writing new pieces. We'd just be getting there, we'd be

reading them on the stage.... We had the chance to be able to hear them as soon as they were written.... Later on, many of these compositions were recorded—by Jimmy with his group, by me with the Giants, and also by the Lighthouse groups.

Howard Rumsey
interview in Jazz Magazine
March 1986

Previn, Norvo, and Basie

Trumpeter Shorty Rogers gives his version of the Sundays at the Lighthouse and discusses his influences.

André Previn initiated me to serial writing. I did a few experiments and it pleased me a lot.... The Giants included Jimmy, Shelly, and myself, then Pete Jolly, and Curtis Counce or Ralph Pena on bass. All three of us liked experimental things.... I'd found little schemes that, to my knowledge, had never been used and certainly not by the dodecaphonic [twelve-tone] composers. It was a question of adapting that system to jazz and of obtaining different harmonic progressions.

Would you call that "free jazz"?

Yes, I believe so. It wasn't completely "free" because we had things written down, but inside of that there were passages where you had to close your eyes, not look at the music any longer in order to play completely free.

In [Red Norvo's] groups there was always something unique: They played softly, delicately, and that ended up by becoming part of me to the point that I was using a mute. Later, without realizing it, we did things that were unusually gentle with the Giants—in fact, it was a bit in the style of Count Basie's Kansas City Seven: little variations on the piano, much *walking bass*, and that sound that has been identified …as the "West Coast sound." But when I look back and ask myself: "Where did I hear that sound? Where does that come from?" I tell myself that it comes from my experience with Red and my love for the Kansas City Seven.…

I've sometimes been called the "father of West Coast jazz," while that really was Norvo and Count Basie.… My only goal was to play and to be pleased with myself. They should really have talked about "pleasing jazz."

Shorty Rogers
interview in *Jazz Magazine*
April 1986

Latin Jazz

Singer-percussionist Machito, trumpeters Mario Bauza and Dizzy Gillespie, bassist Al McKibbon, and arrangers Gil Fuller and George Russell testify to the enthusiasm and the difficulties that often accompanied the meeting of Afro-Cuban and jazz musicians.

All the musicians were crazy about the idea of playing with Charlie Parker. He'd come with the idea of playing "El Manicero" and recording it, but "El Manicero" has something that can't be written…but must be felt.…

In the beginning the jazz musicians had trouble adapting to our rhythms. Often they wouldn't find the downbeat, for we don't play an even 4/4. It must be felt: The bongocero and the timbalero make polyrhythms. The downbeat is there, me, I hear it, but there are many people, even Latins, who don't hear it. We weren't expecting Charlie Parker to play with that Latin feeling. We were expecting his richness from him, his expressiveness. We didn't ask him to adapt himself to us. We adapted ourselves to him. Sometimes we gladly limited ourselves for him. We could have done a million things to throw him off, but that was precisely what we didn't want to do. We wanted him to feel good, and in the end we didn't record "El Manicero."

Machito
interview in *Jazz Magazine*
January 1979

Well, I was the cause of it, that marriage, that integration. I tell you what happened. When Dizzy left Calloway, he told me he wanna do something. I said, "Well, why don't you get on this kick?" We had this idea for a long time. We talked together in the band about it.

So he said, "You got the man?"

"I got the man for you to do that gig." So I got ahold of Chano Pozo who was a friend of mine and another bongo player, and I arranged for them to rehearse with Dizzy. And Dizzy was so enthusiastic, he kept Chano.

Even when Dizzy organized his band with Chano and Max Roach, the drummer used to catch hell trying to

adapt. The conga used to interrupt them, you know, until they found the right kind of approach…between the two countries. It's two countries, but it's the same thing. Every rhythm comes from Africa, and all blacks come from over there, regardless.

Mario Bauza
quoted in Dizzy Gillespie
To Be or Not to Bop
1979

Chano taught us all multirhythm; we learned from the master. On the bus, he'd give me a drum, Al McKibbon a drum, and he'd take a drum. Another guy would have a cowbell, and he'd give everybody a rhythm. We'd see how all the rhythms tied into one another, and everybody was playing something different. We'd be on the road in a bus, riding down the road, and we'd sing and play all down the highway. He'd teach us some of those Cuban chants and things like that. That's how I learned to play the congas. The chants, I mix up. I don't know one from the other, really, but they're all together. You have different ones, the Nañigo, the Ararra, the Santo, and several others, and they each have their own rhythm. When you say do the Nañigo, the guy goes into that specific rhythm. They're all of African derivation.

Dizzy Gillespie
Gillespie, *To Be or Not to Bop*

When I joined the band in the last part of 1947 and really got to know Dizzy and his views on music, the way he felt about African influences and Afro-Cuban influences, he was kind of a revolutionary to me. That really killed me; I was very young then. He knew and still knows where it all came from

you know, African and Afro-Cuban. Everything original that was being done in music was African derivative. So when he got Chano Pozo in the band, that just killed me because I was always intrigued with drums, and to hear a drum played by hand was new to me. I'm from the Midwest, and here is this guy beating this goddam drum with his hands and telling a story. And Dizzy could see him in the band, you know. I couldn't…I couldn't. Hell, man, to me Count Basie's rhythm section was it! Of course, Jimmy Blanton had twisted my head around sideways, but as a rhythm section, I thought Basie's was it. So, anyhow, Dizzy was always that farsighted, that he could see Chano Pozo playing in his band. And I said, "Aww, man, what a drag." But he came in, added another dimension, and was the first in a jazz band, you know, on conga drums. And look what's come of it.

Al McKibbon
Gillespie, *To Be or Not to Bop*

I think the first real Latin thing we did was "Manteca." And we wrote "Manteca" in my apartment, at 94 LaSalle Street, with nobody there but Dizzy, me, Chano, and Bill Graham. Chano would sing you from thing to thing. And what broke up the night was, we asked him, "Whaddayou want the bass to do? Whaddayou think this should be? Whaddayou want the trumpets to do?"

"Pee-de-do! Pee-da-do! Pee-da-do!" Chano was doing that s——.

Finally, I told him, "Hey, O.K., I got enough. Go ahead, I'll fix it." Because we stayed there for about two hours with that kinda s——. As Dizzy said, Chano had some of the figures that he wanted out and out.

We sat down at the piano then, trying to structure the thing. Dizzy sat down at the piano, "How about this?"

So you take the harmonies from Dizzy and say, "We'll fix the rest of it, don't worry!"

When Dizzy said Chano started out with the saxophones, he didn't have that s——. He didn't have none of that. He had that line; he had that melody line. And then he would say, "Pee-do-do! Pee-de-de! Pee-de-do!" That's exactly what he said.

Chano would have ideas for songs. To show you where that was, "Guarachi Guaro" was another type thing that Chano was gonna do. And if you listen to "Guarachi Guaro," it will drive you nuts because it does the same thing all over again because it just keeps going and repeats itself ad infinitum. And it never got off the ground like it should have because it wasn't structured. It wasn't structured in terms of something with form. The form was lacking.

Walter Gilbert Fuller
Gillespie, *To Be or Not to Bop*

Dizzy and I collaborated on "Cubana Be, Cubana Bop," that was in 1947.

Diz had written a sketch which was mostly "Cubana Be." His sketch was what later turned out to be the section of the piece called "Cubana Be" except that I wrote a long introduction to that which was at the time modal. I mean it wasn't based on any chords, which was an innovation in jazz because the modal period didn't really begin to happen until Miles popularized it in 1959. So that piece was written in 1947, and the whole concept of my introduction was modal, and then Dizzy's theme came in and we performed it. Then I wrote the second part, "Cubana Bop." During a bus ride to play at Symphony Hall in Boston, I heard Chano Pozo doing this Nañigo, this Cuban music that was like black mysticism. So I suggested to Dizzy at the time that at the concert that night we open the piece up and have Chano take a solo section by himself. Then we worked it out somehow so the band would come in chanting after Chano, and that was the way the piece went down. Now, actually, Dizzy and I were the writers, but when it began to get to the stage where Victor recorded it, Chano insisted that he also be listed as a composer. Well, in a sense, he's justified because his improvisations in the middle of it were his own things. They weren't written, but they were his own improvisations. So out of respect to Chano, we all agreed that he should be the third party. He was listed as one of the composers.

Diz had a very unique sense of putting chord progressions together, you know, and his theme "Cubana Be, Cubana Bop" was really, really fabulous, amazing for that time. So really imaginative in a harmonic sense.

Chano's concept came from Africa. When I heard it, it sounded on fire to me, the mixing of the standard American drumming together with the Afro-Cuban thing. We were striving for exactly that kind of world grasp, a kind of universality. There were all kinds of influences in that piece, but chief was the melding of the Afro-Cuban and traditional jazz. Not traditional, but the contemporary jazz drumming of the time. So the accent was on rhythm.

George Russell
Gillespie, *To Be or Not to Bop*

Great Figures

Contemporary jazz lovers sometimes feel disoriented and miss the prophets who, in the past, would indicate the road to be followed. The fifties were the last breeding ground for these legendary figures. But a foreshadowing of today's explosion of styles could be seen even then, in the diversity of the musicians' ways and through their questions and contradictions.

Monk's Way

"Error is part of Monk's system." The French composer, novelist, and musicologist André Hodeir describes Thelonious Monk's method: Searching for a chord he has in his head, he comes upon another one by accident, and stays with it.

Does Monk have doubts? Does he suffer? A drop of sweat stood out on his forehead when he played the last quaver of the twenty-first measure.

He knows the rendezvous is imminent. Where? Hasn't he already passed beyond the objective? Not to worry. When? He bends his will. There it is! The sforzando! Dramatic stress! Aaaahhh! A sensational turn of events: Monk didn't play the chord. Another

Thelonious Monk.

Sonny Rollins.

combination happened. His fingers and he himself, one single impulse. Such a beautiful combination, one that corresponds so perfectly to the stress of the phrase that one thing is immediately certain: The other chord, the one Monk wanted to find, was only a preparatory stage, a rough draft of the one he'd just discovered in its overwhelming truth. Monk opens his mouth and a wail escapes him, a cry of triumph. "I've got it! I've got it!"…

Monk can't pursue the goal he'd set himself any longer. A laughable goal! The unexpected chord, the lovely chord, so suddenly emerged, has blown the landscape away in which he used to move around slowly. A new world opens up to him, one that forces a genetic mutation upon him. He changes character. He runs. He leaps. Sometimes his fingers precede him, sometimes he guides them, he runs too fast, he no longer knows what's happening to him, he's reeling with happiness; and at the same time he understands his chance has died. A drop of sweat falls on the piano next to one of his fingers, which stops moving.

He realizes he's stopping, that he has stopped playing. A solitary note, a decapitated ti in B-flat resounds lengthily in the silence that has returned and is barely filled by the purring of the tape recorder busily recording the silence.

André Hodeir
Les Mondes du Jazz
1970

"Sonny the Loner"

After reading journalist and novelist Alain Gerber's liner notes for The Bridge (RCA), it is easier to understand how a figure of the stature of Sonny Rollins might appear as marginal and unclassifiable in a history of jazz.

At the end of the fifties, when Sonny Rollins retires from the jazz stage to meditate and resolve certain philosophical and musical problems, it is because he has been hurt by the rise of Coltrane and feels the need to fertilize a competitive universe. That is the time of the legend: Sonny-the-Wise

Lee Konitz.

reflecting upon the world....

Sonny-the-Mystic is converting to Rosicrucianism, Sonny-the-Loner plays saxophone in the fog on the Williamsburg Bridge. The bridge. *The Bridge.* At the end of 1961 he picks his activities up again, begins by honoring a contract at the Jazz Gallery. In January and February 1962 he makes a recording with Jim Hall, Bob Cranshaw, and Ben Riley (or H. T. Sanders for *God Bless the Child),* the title of which will prove to be a gold mine for specialized journalism. And yet, upon closer examination one notes that Sonny has never crossed a bridge—at least, not in any definitive way—without retracing his steps and revisiting the other shore. He never stopped doing so throughout a very full recording career.

Sonny, or rather his style, remains undiscovered, for this refusal to choose is the man himself.... "Music is of interest to me only as a translation of what I am on the human level." At one time, he thought he was able to conjugate this ill-timed humanity, expel it from an art in which it sows dispersion....

A few months after *The Bridge* is issued, he will be forced to admit that this plurality is not a weakness of his approach but one of its essential determinations. "I try to remain faithful to myself," he laments, "but in spite of myself, I never manage to express myself in the same way." He should rejoice in this, for the exceptional richness of his work is dependent precisely upon the fact that he has never known how to block its dynamism by being fixed on one single project.

Alain Gerber,
liner notes for Sonny Rollins,
The Bridge, RCA

Art Blakey.

"There Is a Jazz of Fire, a Jazz of Fog"

Alain Gerber compares Lee Konitz and Art Blakey, symbols of cool and hard bop.

Arthur loves to play at being the happy native, tribal dances, sounds of the bush, happy revels of the bull in the china shop. Lee does not mind being taken for an intellectual, with his glasses, ranking first with Lennie Tristano, a fish in water among the super subtle geometrics of Martial Solal. Blakey breaks the whole kit and caboodle; Konitz could reconstruct the world on the head of a pin. At least the roles are carefully divided.

For almost half a century, Abdullah Ibn Buhaina praises the Lord with shattering cymbals, his skull a little cracked by a blow received in a raid on Arabs. When the others are cooking up bop in their witches' cauldrons in the pantry, he's bustling about in the cellar, obstinately nailing down who knows what weird and startling piece. From time to time, without giving any warning, he rushes ahead with a bucket of charcoal and empties it in the stairwell.

Vrrrrooommmmmmm! He's happy as a lark, that guy. He limps around like Vulcan and, pretending to be the derelict locomotive mechanic run wild, mouth open, eyes rolled back, he has never missed the tiniest shift. Art Blakey, escapee from the bamboo hut, is the most secure man of jazz; he is the one whom you could ask for the secret of swing were you to have lost it in the men's room at the Poughkeepsie station.

All that time, very humble and quite pale, Lee Konitz blows bits of fog from the corner of his mouth. He knows the music so well that he can forget everything and leave for elsewhere. He's never denied himself this. He's the man who goes off into dreamland. The absentee. The motionless traveler, visitor of countries that don't exist, that are shadows and mysteries, and fleeting glimmers of light.

He too, though, knows exactly what he's doing. In this world, the beauty of jazz remains a crime without excuse: premeditated relapse.

Alain Gerber
Le Matin
14 May 1982

Bill Evans and John Coltrane, Innovators

Miles Davis introduces the two musicians who influenced his adoption of modal jazz.

Trane was the loudest, fastest saxophonist I've ever heard. He could play real fast and real loud at the same time and that's very difficult to do. Because when most players play loud, they lock themselves. I've seen many saxophonists get messed up trying to play like that. But Trane could do it and he was phenomenal. It was like he was possessed when he put that horn in his mouth. He was so passionate—fierce—and yet so quiet and gentle when he wasn't playing. A sweet guy.

He scared me one time while we were in California when he wanted to go to the dentist to get a tooth put in. Trane could play two notes all at once, and I thought his missing tooth was the cause of it. I thought it gave him his sound. … I almost panicked. I told him that I had called a rehearsal for the same time that he was going. I asked him if he could postpone his dental appointment. "Naw," he said, "naw, man, I can't make the rehearsal; I'm going to the dentist." I asked him what kind of replacement he was going to get and he says, "A permanent one," So I try to talk him into getting a removable one that he can take out every night before he plays. He looks at me like I'm crazy. He goes to the dentist and comes back looking like a piano, he was grinning so much. At the gig that night—I think it was at the Blackhawk—I play my first solo and go back by Philly Joe and wait for Trane to play, almost in tears because I know he's f—— himself up. But when he ripped off them runs like he always did, man, talk about a m—— being relieved!...

After Red Garland walked out on me, I found a new piano player named Bill Evans.... I needed a piano player who was into the modal thing, and Bill Evans was. I met Bill Evans through George Russell, whom Bill had studied with. I knew George from the days back at Gil's house on 55th Street. As I was getting deeper into the modal thing, I asked George if he knew a piano player who could play the kinds of things I wanted, and he recommended Bill....

Bill brought a great knowledge of classical music, people like Rachmaninoff and Ravel.... Bill had this quiet fire that I loved on piano. The way he approached it, the sound he got was like crystal notes or sparkling water cascading down from some clear waterfall. I had to change the way the band sounded again for Bill's style by playing different tunes, softer ones at first. Bill played underneath the rhythm, and I liked that, the way he played scales with the band. Red's playing had carried the rhythm but Bill underplayed it and for what I was doing now with the modal thing, I liked what Bill was doing better.

Miles Davis
Miles, the Autobiography

John Coltrane.

From Free Jazz to Third World Music

With free jazz, African-American music attempted to liberate itself from the models presented by white culture. Beyond the dead end, where the adventure ran out and beyond the rebirth of the black avant-garde in the sixties, there was still an opportunity for multiple questions, which elicited responses from Paris to Buenos Aires.

Free Jazz/Black Power

The role of the improvisations, their place, their status no longer have much to do with the all-time traditions: Most often, all the musicians of a group improvise together and each on his own. This restoration of the principles of collective improvisation inscribes black American music once again with what the critics have called "New Orleans polyphony."

"We try," [Albert] Ayler used to say, "to rejuvenate that old feeling from New Orleans that music can be played collectively and freely."

Furthermore, even when they succeed each other in time, free jazz improvisations add themselves on to each other, oppose each other, consist of networks, strata, layers of resonant lines—rather than the same line prolonged by several musicians taking over from each other. Thus the whole work becomes an improvisation to the extent that its structure, its form as a whole is born from the more or less expected interchange of the individual lines.

Polycentric, free collective improvisation is in fact much more than the mere reactivation of the polyphonic system of New Orleans jazz.... Its nature is essentially uncertain: provocative, risky, playful. Many musicians of free jazz affirm that it isn't necessary to go through academic Western training in order to play Afro-American music.... Whence

Albert Ayler.

comes an often rather unorthodox use of the instruments, a need to go beyond the instrumental limits imposed by Western norms.

What used to be an accident or exception becomes a new resonant possibility: The whistling of the reed (yesterday erased from Charlie Parker's records as mistakes) is now accepted, validated as an integral part of the discourse; the effects of breath, the noises until now considered to be parasites of resonant purity are exploited, worked in; an "elsewhere" (high-pitched registers, "incongruous" sounds, banging the saxophone keys, and so forth) of the usual field of action is elicited continuously.… Ayler affirms that the sounds become more important than the notes and henceforth the musician seems not to care whether the notes be considered "good" or "bad." Cries, sounds, clashes, growling, gnashing: All the infra-musical effects participate in the discourse of the improviser.

Philippe Carles and
Jean-Louis Comolli,
Free Jazz/Black Power,
1979

Albert Ayler's Cry

From the pen of the French poet and critic Jacques Réda, an analysis.

How to end it? One doesn't know. And one doesn't know because one doesn't want to. Nobody really wants to end. When you're at the end of a blind alley, what do you do? Other than delight in it and find a certain accomplishment in it, you could sit down and decide to keep quiet; or tell yourself under your breath that you're somewhere else and manage to believe that; or retrace your steps in order to try and find some opening somewhere; or take refuge in your memories; or hit your head against a wall; or both at the same time; or imagine that you're going to get up and escape up high; or pray that the end may come quickly which, since you're addressing it to someone who has power over it, will therefore not really be the end; or set your hand at successful results. You could also deny the end or begin to howl until it occurs.

That is how Albert Ayler experienced the end of jazz. Not only by howling, by remembering, by praying, by hitting his head against a wall, and by running in every direction, but by hastening it with artless joy. More ardently and candidly than anyone else did he carry this test through to the end. Undoubtedly not through a perverse lyrical exaltation, but because he, too, refused it, considering that every end has a double reason for existence, that there is no end without the possibility of a new beginning. What he knocked his head against was therefore not an insuperable limit but the inert and endless space that the end may also be, into which only phantoms move forward, and which is populated only by demons, sorcerers, spirits, vibrations. Transported by panic, he pushed them all ahead of him. In order to bear it, he intoned hymns and beat out military marches, murmured drunken lullabies and hiccuped love songs. Always mixing everything and stirring it up so that the end would cough up, suffocate, debase itself, and rip the inaugural truth of a scream from its vacuum.

Jacques Réda
L'Improviste, Une Lecture du Jazz
1990

An Instrument Close to the Voice

The tenor saxophone becomes the king of jazz instruments.

The saxophone…is a very malleable instrument, extremely close to the human voice. And then it is also an instrument without much of a past.

As for me, I consider it a part of my body, an extension of me, I can make it wail, scream, moan.… Free jazz for me is the beginning of the reign of the saxophone, and more specifically of the tenor saxophone.

Michel Portal
in *Jazz Hot*
May–June 1968

The Loft Generation

Living in lofts, if you will, is a life-style. Abandoned studios, factory remnants, stores transformed into single-room places with a suspended bed, white wood furniture and green plants. Or in concert-rehearsal halls.… But in Soho, the Village, the lofts are also a gentler way in which to perceive life, it is a network of less isolated relationships, less neurotic than in the big cities, a true effervescence, a real movement in which a public and the papers participate, as well as a thousand musicians who couldn't be more different and many of whom are well-known—and have been for a long time.… So, whether it is good or not, this movement exists and the records made at Rivbea *(Wildflowers)* were not a mirage. What simply began one day at Rivbea (Sam and Beatrice Rivers), at Artist House (Ornette Coleman), or at the Studio We, what took about ten years to assert itself… is suddenly proliferating, organizing, ramifying; and with jubilation and incontestable success.… And this movement is not a question of musical "style." Its unity stems rather from its lack of conformity.

Francis Marmande
"Transamerica Express"
in *Jazz Magazine*
October 1977

Samuel and Beatrice Rivers.

At the end of a long European stay, the veteran drummer of "the new thing,"

Sunny Murray, discovered the legacy of free jazz in the loft generation.

Like that of bebop, like every musical revolution, the revolution of the avant-garde was a seething mass of exaggerations. We tackled the essence, wasting strength and talent without counting instead of exploiting the results of our ideas.… It is no longer that atmosphere of destructive competition that we once knew, Archie, myself, Rashied Ali, all those from the avant-garde.… I found a new, fresh, lively music here. The music didn't stop a decade ago.…

Sunny Murray
in *Jazz Magazine*
June 1977

Better known for his activities in the world of fusion, the trumpet player Randy Brecker sheds light on some underestimated aspects of the loft scene.

I was twenty-one years old then, and in Manhattan the loft scene was very active, concentrated in three specific buildings. I had my own loft with musicians like Dave Holland, John Abercrombie, Ralph Towner, Stanley Clarke, and Lenny White.… We recorded plenty of cassettes. In the bass player Gene Perla's loft, guys from Boston gathered, such as Don Alias and Jan Hammer. Chick Corea lived on the same floor as my brother Mike. It was always one constant jam session in these three buildings: Often at Mike's place you could hear several jam sessions at the same time on every floor. In the beginning it was primarily free jazz under the influence of Corea, Dave Holland, and Barry Altschul. As for me, I'd come there to play every style of

S̲unny Murray.

music without any preconceived ideas. I'm a trumpet player, not an ideologue! One evening in the late sixties, I was playing free style with Corea and his group, the next day fusion with [Larry] Coryell, or "standard" in the big bands to earn a little money.

Randy Brecker
in *Jazz Hot*
September–October 1982

On the Edge of Free Jazz

Even though they were strangers to the free movement, Miles' companions knew how to listen to it and draw inferences from it. Herbie Hancock remembers his encounter with Eric Dolphy very well.

I answered him very frankly that I wasn't sure I could play that kind of music: "What am I supposed to play? Are there any melodic lines, any chords in this music?" He answered me: "Of course, we have our own melodies and our chords." I could hardly get over it.

It sounded so free.... He told me to play exactly as I felt it. Before the first evening I was still perplexed. I decided to take this approach: I wouldn't count on the rules I normally followed—I would replace them with new rules that would make my playing freer.... Sometimes, because I'd overstep the bounds, I'd be completely lost; but then I learned there was no harm in that. The important thing is to listen carefully to what the others are playing and to arrive at creating something that can be integrated into the context without worrying about the rest, the base structures of the piece....

Tony Williams had belonged to various avant-garde groups; he had already worked with Sam Rivers in Boston when he was about fourteen or fifteen. What they used to play then was very much ahead of its time. When he composed the music of "Spring" and "Life Time," he asked me to write it down since he wasn't able to do so: He'd play the notes with two fingers on the piano.... They were always astonishing melodies, strange rhythms.... He didn't speak in terms of notes or chords.... It was a new way of thinking about the elaboration of music, a little like one might approach putting a painting together in terms of forms, colors, and so on. That, too, is an avant-garde concept I discovered with him.

Herbie Hancock
in *Jazz Hot*
July–August 1979

Tony Williams' Point of View

I don't really see the point in a drummer continuously playing high hat from one end of a piece to the other.... My tempo is in my head and, I hope, in my cymbals. You might say that I place myself in the category of drummers who play "free," a word I don't much care for. Most of the drummers who play that way no longer mark time.... For me, rhythmic permanence is a certain feeling, a particular sound quality which you can get just as well on the cymbals. This tempo is inside me and so at the end of my sticks; I feel it and one must notice it.

Tony Williams
in *Jazz Magazine*
June 1965

Wayne Shorter on Miles Davis

In public, yes [Miles plays free]. Maybe on the records it can't be heard that well, though undoubtedly the reaching-out toward a certain freedom can be grasped there.... But in public we used to really play very free, especially with the group that included Jack DeJohnette and Chick Corea and even with Tony Williams and Herbie Hancock.

Wayne Shorter
in *Jazz Magazine*
November 1971

Identity Crisis

Free jazz made an indelible mark on jazz musicians around the world, leaving them wondering about their true identity. French musician Michel Portal was one of the first to ask these questions. Later he would be one of the first to respond.

For us the drama is that we are playing stolen music. It is black music, born in a specific context, as a reaction to a specific political and ideological situation.... And then there is the problem of cultural roots. We don't pick up a guitar at fourteen and we don't start singing the blues.... I'd like to play music that would correspond to [Albert Ayler] for France. But for now it isn't easy to find what that might be.

Michel Portal
in *Jazz Hot*
May–June 1968

Gato Barbieri.

The Musical Wealth of the Developing World

For the sax player Gato Barbieri the answer lies in returning to Argentina.

I no longer wanted to play music that didn't belong to me. I was going through a crisis period and didn't know what to do any more.... That's when I met up with the Brazilian director Glauber Rocha again.... Glauber is very sensitive to everything concerning the Third World.... He told me: "You come from an underdeveloped country, you belong to a subculture: You must do something that starts with what you know. You should be proud of it and not try to do or play what you've learned through colonialism any longer.... You must work on what is best in you, most true, on what you have that is profoundly Latin American." I began to think of a recording on which I'd play music I had a memory of. For example, the *Bachianas Brasileiras* of Villa-Lobos, melodies I'd heard as a kid.... In Argentina, I played with folkloric musicians.... There I found my roots again without going through any complex intellectual process, and my relationship with jazz became necessarily more abstract, more intellectualized.... I understood quite well why there'd be no jazz in Brazil: Popular music there is so fantastic and rich. It was their jazz—a little like the tango for the Argentines.

Gato Barbieri
in *Jazz Magazine*
February 1972

Jazz Is Plugged In

Miles Davis and other jazz musicians came face-to-face with rock and roll in the late 1960s. Davis was one of the first jazz players to draw lessons from this encounter. With jazz-rock, new sounds, new styles of playing, and new methods of recording all appeared.

A Sound Plus Rock

In February 1969 Miles Davis takes a new turn with In a Silent Way.

I first met Jimi [Hendrix] when his manager called up and wanted me to introduce him to the way I was playing and putting my music together. Jimi liked what I had done on *Kind of Blue* and some other stuff and wanted to add more jazz elements to what he was doing. He liked the way Coltrane played with all those sheets of sound, and he played the guitar in a similar way. Plus, he said he had heard the guitar voicing that I used in the way I played the trumpet. So we started getting together....

He was a real nice guy, quiet but intense, and was nothing like people thought he was. He was just the opposite of the wild and crazy image he presented on the stage. When we started getting together and talking about music, I found out that he couldn't read music....

There are a lot of great musicians who don't read music—black and white—that I have known and respected and played with. So I didn't think less of

Joe Zawinul.

Jimi because of that. Jimi was just a great, natural musician—self-taught....

[Later, in a recording session] we changed what Joe [Zawinul] had written on "In a Silent Way," cut down all the chords and took his melody and used that. I wanted to make the sound more like rock. In rehearsals we had played it like Joe had written it, but it wasn't working for me because all the chords were cluttering it up. I could hear that the melody that Joe had written—which was hidden by all the other clutter—was really beautiful. When we recorded I just threw out the chord sheets and told everyone to play just the melody, just to play off that....

I had been experimenting with writing a few simple chord changes for three pianos. Simple s——, and it was funny because I used to think when I was doing them how Stravinsky went back to simple forms. So I had been writing these things down, like one beat chord and a bass line, and I found out that the more we played it, it was always different. I would write a chord, a rest, maybe another chord, and it turned out that the more it was played, the more it just kept getting different. This started happening in 1968 when I had Chick, Joe, and Herbie for those studio dates. It went on into the sessions we had for *In a Silent Way*. Then I started thinking about something larger, a skeleton of a piece. I would write a chord on two beats and they'd have two beats out. So they would do one, two, three, da-dum, right? Then I put the accent on the fourth beat. Maybe I had three chords on the first bar. Anyway, I told the musicians that they could do anything they wanted, play

anything they heard but that I had to have this, what they did, as a chord. Then they knew what they could do, so that's what they did. Played off that chord, and it made it sound like a whole lot of stuff.

I told them that at rehearsals and then I brought in these musical sketches that nobody had seen, just like I did on *Kind of Blue* and *In a Silent Way*. We started early in the day in Columbia's studio on 52nd Street and recorded all day for three days in August. I had told Teo Macero, who was producing the record, to just let the tapes run and get everything we played, told him to get *everything* and not to be coming in interrupting, asking questions....

So I would direct, like a conductor, once we started to play, and I would either write down some music for somebody or I would tell him to play different things I was hearing, as the music was growing, coming together. It was loose and tight at the same time. It was casual but alert, everybody was alert to different possibilities that were coming up in the music....

Sometimes, instead of just letting the tape run, I would tell Teo to back it up so I could hear what we had done. If I wanted something else in a certain spot, I would just bring the musician in, and we would just do it.

Miles Davis
Miles, the Autobiography

Sketches by Weather Report

In an interview, Wayne Shorter compares Miles Davis' work methods with those of the group Weather Report in its early stages.

When you would bring new compositions for Miles' band, how would that happen?

In fact, we never really rehearsed. I'd arrive at the studio with my scores and we'd play them in different ways—the arrangements were open enough to do that.... It's a little as if I weren't using punctuation, commas, question marks....

It's a completely different formula from the traditional "song form," a formula that must allow for the widest movements in its center.

And with Weather Report?

We trace some sketches, we express ideas, and we rehearse because we've chosen to take our time and to rehearse. We work those ideas, we see what each one can make of them.

Josef, Miroslav, and I write for the group, both together and separately, but the final product is a collective one: Each one of us listens to the ideas of the others, the way in which he plays them.

Do you always use chord patterns for improvisation?

No, there are no preset chords. We put together something that resembles a script in filigree, that can be modified according to the feeling of the moment. We try not to build something too logical.

Wayne Shorter
in *Jazz Magazine*
November 1971

John Scofield Looks Back

John Scofield, who played guitar for Miles Davis in the eighties, presents some

John Scofield.

details on the recording session of Decoy *(1984). Comparing it to his own album* Electric Outlet *of the same year, he discusses the evolution of working in the studio.*

This theme *(What It Is)* was born in the studio. Miles always started every take all alone. We must have done about ten of them with a slow blues feeling—this is not on the recording. But that solo intro there gave us *Robot 415,* which was later picked up again and redone.

Gil Evans arrived that day with some music. He said: "You recognize it? That's what you played last night with Miles." Miles had us work chord passages, from do seventh to fa seventh, then with a little bridge

from mi seventh to mi B-flat seventh,
from re seventh to sol seventh.
Then, without my knowing it, he
gave the tape to Gil and said to him:
"Transcribe what John played in certain
passages." For almost two hours we
worked it over and over again....

I'd do a solo, then Miles would play,
then Branford Marsalis had a solo,
Miles would play again, we'd play the
melody, and so forth. Then we'd stop,
he'd listen to the takes and would say:
"Good, let's try that...."

*Please explain how your methods differ
from Miles'.*

Miles plays with the group, and then
he adds a few touches. *Electric Outlet*
was really made very differently. I
started it at home, recording a guitar
and bass part with a rhythm box. Then
I redid it in the studio. And then we
added a real drummer, a real
synthesizer, and real winds: Dave
Sanborn and Ray Anderson.

*So Steve Jordan played, although the tape
had already been recorded?*

Exactly. There was a rhythm box in
his place on that tape, but on certain
others we left the bass drum and the
snare drum in order to deepen the
back beat. The process can become
mechanical, very cold, but we tried to
loosen it up. If I had an idea, I'd play it.
Steve reacted to an idea I'd had the
night before. The saxophone player
reacted to what Steve was playing. This
recording rests for 50 percent on the
reaction the musicians had to one
another—live it's 100 percent, but
there, obviously, the person on the tape
couldn't react.

For me, whether it's a tape or a
group, I do the same thing. I simply try
to play the present moment. And I
always play with people, the fact they've
been prerecorded changes nothing.
When I close my eyes in the studio,
when I have the headset on, it makes no
difference whether the drummer is
there or not.

John Scofield
in *Jazz Magazine*
May 1991

The Fender Piano

*Miles Davis and Herbie Hancock describe
the introduction of the Fender piano into
their music.*

I had a bass line in my head with
the voicings Gil [Evans] used with his
big band.... It wasn't only that I
wanted to get into electronic music as
many have said, supposedly because
I had some electronic stuff in the
group. I was looking for a voicing
that a Fender-Rhodes, not a piano,
could bring me. Same for the bass;
musicians should use instruments
that best reflect their period, the
technology that will give them what
they want to hear.

Miles Davis
in *Jazz Hot*
Summer 1983

It was during a session with Miles: The
only keyboard there was a Fender-
Rhodes. I asked Miles: "What do you
want me to play?" He answered in a
hoarse voice: "Play that...."

Not only had I never played it before,
but someone had told me some
disconcerting stuff about this gadget. I
try it anyway, I hit a chord—and
whoa!—it sounded so warm, so

Steve Swallow.

harmonious, so rich that I adopted it immediately.

Then I got to the wa-wa pedal and used an Echoplex echo chamber by taking the Fender's cover off to find a place to plug them in: At the time it hadn't been made to do that.

The music we used to make was avant-garde but a combination of several styles as well, and so covered a rather wide musical field. So I realized that I needed more sounds, which sometimes led me to play on the Rhodes' resonators with drumsticks.... I remember that Harold Rhodes came to see us several times and, noticing all these weird hookups, asked me: "What have you done to it?" From that moment on these pianos were equipped with jacks for these effects. I also suggested that an output be installed for the studio, for more and more musicians felt a need for it.

Herbie Hancock
in Jazz Hot
Summer 1983

From the Double Bass to the Electric Bass

For some musicians using an electric bass was an opportunity to open up to new kinds of music.

I used to listened only to Paul Chambers, Percy Heath, etc., but when I moved on to the electric bass I discovered other kinds of music I began to like. So much so that the records I presently buy are essentially not jazz records but soul music.... First I listened to Marvin Gaye to hear Jamerson, then I began to pay more attention to Marvin Gaye than to his bass player, and I discovered another kind of music I love just as much as jazz now. Another reference for me is Larry Graham, the bass player of Sly and the Family Stone.

Steve Swallow
in *Jazz Magazine*
September 1986

The Breckers' Way

Randy Brecker: Mike and I were very influenced by [Larry] Coryell's first record with Bob Moses and Jim Pepper, under the name the Free Spirits. It was a kind of jazzified country-rock with interesting lyrics. A very good record. It was at that time that the group Dreams was born; Mike and his musicians had jammed and been joined by Billy Cobham. It went well and it was suggested to us we work to put together a regular group. [John] Abercrombie joined us shortly thereafter.

Michael Brecker: Jim Pepper is a Creek Indian who recorded very little. He has a tremendous sound and plays quite free, a little like Dewey Redman. I'd just finished university, I was playing a lot of rock 'n roll at the time, and that record made me think. Suddenly I understood some things because of Pepper's ideas and phrasing.

"Tenor Rock 'n Roll"

At the end of the sixties, the guitar became very important. Michael Brecker was influenced primarily by guitar players and singers.

I was one of the few who played "tenor rock 'n roll." It was a wide open field.... I enjoyed playing something other than pure bebop, transposing bop things for

rock 'n roll.... I grew up with all that music. At home, there was always jazz and rock 'n roll. At the time I was heavily influenced by guitar players like B. B. King, Albert King, Eric Clapton, and Hendrix, who to me is a genius. It was a very exciting period when we created the group Dreams, with Cobham, Abercrombie, and the others. In that period of mixing jazz and rock 'n roll, a saxophone player had a wide open road: In that context I was able to find an original sound while, when playing jazz, I was merely a depreciated Coltrane....

Weren't you also listening to blues saxophone players like A. C. Reed?

No, I was listening to the guitar players; they were the ones who really did it at the time in that kind of music. Everything that didn't come from bebop was in the phrasings of the guitar players and the singers. And in my subconscious all that melted together. I never wanted to sound like a bebop musician.

Michael Brecker
in *Jazz Hot*
September–October 1982

Michael and Randy Brecker.

Jazz Overseas

Outside the United States, no country has welcomed jazz more fervently than France. Its history there is almost as long and as rich as it is on this side of the Atlantic.

Swing Waltzes and Hot Jazz

During the First World War American troops entered France with recordings of a new type of music stashed in their baggage.

As soon as the conflict was over, the Paris stage reached out to black musicians. Performing out of the music halls, such musicians as Hugues Panassié and Charles Delaunay were extremely popular. In 1935 Delaunay created *Jazz Hot*, which was the first jazz journal in the world.

At that same time, with Jean Sablon and especially Charles Trenet, the French song became swing. In fact, the whole French music hall changed. Authentic jazz musicians took over entire instrumental sections—often even the conductor's spot—in orchestra pits. This is how the bands of Jacques Hélian, Ray Ventura, and Alix Combelle were born.

In the recording studios, French instrumentalists sometimes had the opportunity to match their talents with those of the black American musicians who were passing through. But French musicians were not at the forefront of jazz until the guitar player Django Reinhardt arrived. Trained in the popular dance hall and the gypsy styles, Reinhardt was the first to use the syntax of American blacks to the benefit of an original musical language. With the violinist Stéphane Grappelli, he created the Quintette du Hot Club de France, without brass or

Django Reinhardt: The beginnings of a true French jazz.

drums. Thus Reinhardt (with his followers, the brothers Matelo, Sarane, and Baro Ferret) and Grappelli (with his immediate competitor Michel Warlop) were at the roots of a French tradition of "jazz for strings" that continues today.

In Saint-Germain-des-Prés

After four years of isolation during World War II, France enthusiastically embraced the returning American jazz musician.

A new style had appeared that nobody knew anything about. The battle of "real jazz" (the supporters of the New Orleans revival) vs. the bop style, which Charles Delaunay, Boris Vian, and composer André Hodeir defended in the magazine *Jazz Hot*, was waged in a France largely loyal to traditional American models until well into the sixties.

Some Americans (Lester Young, Bud Powell) played regularly in the Saint-Germain-des-Prés area of Paris, and others even settled in France (Sidney Bechet, Kenny Clarke). They found some excellent sidemen among the French jazz players.

Some of these sidemen managed to blossom within the framework of the orthodoxy of American jazz, but others obviously aspired to detach themselves from it and forge new ways of playing. André Hodeir and the piano player Martial Solal became internationally known because of their completely personal styles.

Free Jazz in the Family

In the sixties, with the onslaught of rock and roll, jazz fell out of fashion with young people.

Martial Solal, an original voice.

In France as in the United States, free jazz rejected both the old rules and the old idols. Not only did it mesh with the interests of a generation in rebellion, but in France it also fed into a movement for another type of freedom, encouraging the musicians to break away from their big brothers in America. Young French musicians were attracted to the big groups of Jef Gilson, the New Thing, and, soon, the electronic bands of Miles Davis. But what interested them more than a precise vocabulary was a certain independent spirit. After 1968 there were an increasing number of group experiments with improvisation (the Cohelmec Ensemble, the Dharma Quintet, the Workshop de Lyon).

The disappearance of rules and the diversification of practices fragmented jazz into various families. Deprived of structures that used to allow for jam sessions, impromptu encounters became rare but intense. Group improvisation became the quest, often guided by dramatic art, for a terrain of affinities or an imaginary folklore.

A true "theater of the souls," improvisation then tended to concretize its dramatic character through actions onstage that became systematized in the course of the seventies, notably with the Compagnie Lubat.

Crossroads

The diversification of French jazz.

By the end of the seventies everything had changed; jazz even began to share its motivations with the "autonomous" movement and the punk generation. Maintaining relationships of various sorts with free jazz, other musicians trod more classical paths.

Jean-Luc Ponty renewed the use of the violin, beginning in the sixties, by electrifying it and adapting his playing to the Coltranian inheritance. He soon disappeared from France, involved in an American career, but not without having inspired a renewed tradition of strings in jazz; it found a second breath in the work of the Swing

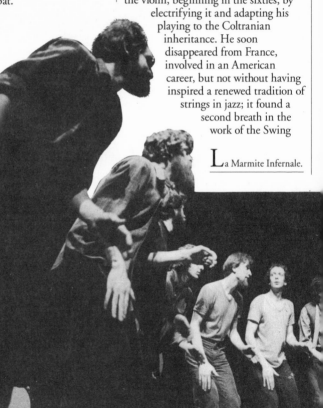

La Marmite Infernale.

Strings System of Didier Levallet.

The accordion once again began to be talked about on the French jazz stage (Marcel Azzola, Richard Galliano, Francis Varis).

Equally outside of any category, Eddy Louiss became known as one of the great masters of the Hammond organ with his music, which was colored with reminiscences of his native Caribbean.

To illustrate his shouting about the quality of the French stage, Daniel Humair displayed his shows of genius on the drums with the older musicians (French or American) or with free jazz musicians. He enjoyed the confrontation with the free jazz musicians, even though he hardly shared their options. With the saxophone player François Jenneau and the bassist Henri Texier, Humair found a balance between the permanent renewal of free improvisation and a rigor that is too often absent from free jazz. Many foreign free jazz musicians of the sixties—like Jean-François Jenny-

Henri Texier.

Clark, Aldo Romano, or the German piano player Joachim Kühn—shared these concerns.

At the end of the seventies great figures who had disappeared in the sixties, such as the piano player René Urtreger, came back to the stage. This return corresponded to the advent of a neoclassical jazz, neither orthodox nor avant-garde, which often expressed itself in small combos (duos or trios) in tiny clubs where drums were forbidden because they'd cause a late-night disturbance: the bass-guitar (Patrice Caratini and Marc Fosset) and piano-bass (François Couturier and Jean-Paul Céléa) duos, the various ensembles of the guitar player Christian Escoudé and of the piano player Michel Graillier. Appearing at the dawn of the eighties, the young Michel Petrucciani very quickly abandoned such intimacy for a roaring transatlantic career. But the heritage of bop continued to be revisited in Parisian clubs.

The Savoy Generation

On the eve of the eighties, big bands were reborn at the same time that a pronounced taste for writing underwent a renaissance.

In 1986 the proliferation of talents in this domain (Antoine Hervé, Laurent Cugny, Luc Le Masne, Denis Badault) motivated the French government to create the Orchestre National de Jazz (ONJ), a move that clearly indicated the state's interest in jazz since 1981. Already troubled by the retreat of free jazz, the experts were intrigued by this suddenly institutionalized jazz, taught in many schools. The breakdown of the barriers between genres also meant that a growing number of musicians practiced improvisation as they came out of their conservatory studies, with never-failing technique and cultural baggage that was more rock than jazz.

The New Generation

The new faces on the French scene, both in and out of the clubs.

Zool Fleischer: Music influenced by Miles Davis.

Laurent Cugny and Gil Evans.

A new generation is emerging, essentially Parisian, trained in the early eighties in the competitive clubs in the capital, such as the Savoy. Geared more toward the art of Miles Davis or Wayne Shorter, pop music, or the ECM productions than toward free jazz or bop, they are, for example, guitar players Marc Ducret, Malo Vallois, Serge Lazarévitch, and Lionel Benhamou; piano players Zool Fleischer, Antoine Hervé, and Andy Emler; saxophone player Eric Barret; trumpet players François Chassagnite and Antoine Illouz; trombone player Denis Leloup; drummers Peter Gritz and Tony Rabeson; bass players Michel Benita and Marc Michel; and percussionist François Verly.

Very much present in the French press, for a long time academic criticism proved to be condescending to this family of musicians that invested in the ONJ. Some critics found them too slick and preferred the heirs of the free jazz movement, who thrived outside the Parisian clubs.

A Certain Ecumenism

In the course of the eighties, the distinction some had made between "creators" and "technicians" lost all its meaning.

The practitioners of free jazz were not exempt from these clichés and schemes, but since the arrival of the clarinet player Louis Sclavis in the ONJ, real talents have been unveiled there: Guitar players Claude Barthélémy (who became the director of the ONJ in 1989) and Philippe Deschepper, trombone player Yves Robert, drummer Gérard Siracusa, and bass player Bruno Chevillon.

More importantly, in many cases, members of the two generations have gained mutual respect as well as communal aspirations that lead them to many collaborative efforts.

Multi-Jazz

Today musicians from many nations meet on the Parisian stage.

There have always been American jazz musicians in Paris, but today they have been joined by musicians of every nationality who have let themselves be lured away from home by the vitality of the Parisian stage. Italians (double bass player Riccardo Del Fra), Danes (saxophone player Simon Spang-Hanssen), Yugoslavians (piano player Bojan Zulfikarpasic), Brazilians, Africans (saxophone player Manu Dibango), West Indians (piano player Michel Sardaby), Argentines (the trios of Mosalini-Beytelmann-Caratini or Gubitsch-Calo-Céléa), and Turks (Senem Diyici) have all contributed to diversifying a French musical landscape, the exhaustive description of which cannot be given in these few lines.

For a long time, these exchanges with other countries were a one-way street, but today, the contacts maintained by Dominique Pifarély and Jean-Paul Céléa and the musicians of the Vienna Art Orchestra, for example, are indicative of a new cooperative situation in which France is recognized as never before.

The recent rise of the Trio Machado, of the Trio à Boum, or of the Patrick Fradet Quartet and the appearance of young musicians destined to fall in step with them, such as the guitar players Noël Akchoté, Eric Löhrer, and David Chevallier, or the saxophone players Julien Loureau and Laurent Dehors, leave one to believe that jazz in France is something to be watched.

Franck Bergerot
and Arnaud Merlin,
1991

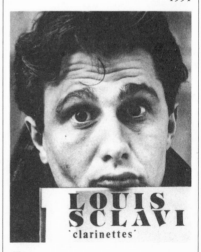

LOUIS SCLAVI
'clarinettes'

Louis Sclavis.

Michel Portal performing with Jean-François Jenny-Clark and Daniel Humair (above), and with his instruments (below).

Discography

Below is a listing of recordings to complement the reading of this book.

With the appearance of the long-playing record (and then, obviously, the compact disk), an artist's oeuvre was no longer dispersed across innumerable sides of 78s; almost every recorded title is now a part of a longer album. However, certain pieces still remain difficult to locate.

CHAPTER I
WHAT TO MAKE OF BEBOP?

Baker, Chet, and Gerry Mulligan, *Baker & Mulligan*, Prestige

Davis, Miles, *The Birth of the Cool*, Capitol, 1949–50

Desmond, Paul, *The Best of Paul Desmond*, Columbia Jazz Contemporary Masters, 1972–5

Getz, Stan, *The Roost Quartets*, Roulette Jazz, 1950–1

———, *Stan Getz Plays*, Verve, 1952–4

Herman, Woody, *Early Autumn, Featuring Stan Getz*, Bluebird, 1976

———, *The Third Herd "Early Autumn,"* Discovery, 1952–4

Lewis, John (Modern Jazz Quartet), *Concorde*, Fantasy/OJC, 1955

Manne, Shelly, *The Three & The Two*, Fantasy/OJC, 1954

Rogers, Shorty, *Modern Sounds*, Capitol

Tristano, Lennie, *Continuity* (Quartet performances with Henry Grimes, Warne Marsh, Paul Motian; quintet performances with Sonny Dallas, Lee Konitz, Warne Marsh, Nick Stabulas), Jazz Records, 1964

CHAPTER II
TOWARD HARD BOP AND MODAL JAZZ

Blakey, Art, *Moanin'*, Blue Note, 1958

Brown, Clifford, and Max Roach, *At Basin Street*, EmArcy, mid-1950s

———, *Study in Brown*, EmArcy, 1956

Dameron, Tadd, *Fontainebleau*, Fantasy/OJC, 1956

Davis, Miles, *Cookin' With the Miles Davis Quintet*, Fantasy/OJC, 1956

———, *Green Haze* (with John Coltrane), Prestige, 1955

———, *Modern Jazz Giants* (with Thelonious Monk), Fantasy/OJC

Evans, Bill, *Everybody Digs Bill Evans*, Fantasy/OJC, 1958

Gillespie, Dizzy, *Dizzy Gillespie & His Big Band*, GNP Crescendo

Hancock, Herbie, *Inventions and Dimensions*, Blue Note

Monk, Thelonious, *The Complete Riverside Recordings*, Riverside, 1955–61

Monk, Thelonious, and Gerry Mulligan, *'Round Midnight* (an anthology), Milestone, 1957

Navarro, Fats, *The Amazing Bud Powell*, Blue Note, 1949–51

Silver, Horace, *Horace Silver & The Jazz Messengers*, Blue Note, mid-1950s

———, *Song For My Father*, Blue Note, 1963–4

Smith, Jimmy, *The Sermon*, Blue Note, 1957–8

CHAPTER III
THE ROAD TO FREEDOM

Art Ensemble of Chicago, *Nice Guys*, ECM, 1978

Ayler, Albert, *Live in Greenwich Village*, MCA/Impulse, 1967–8

Barbieri, Gato, *The Third World Revisited*, Bluebird

Braxton, Anthony, *Creative Orchestra*, Bluebird

Cherry, Don, *Complete Communion*, Blue Note

Coleman, Ornette, *The Shape of Jazz to Come*, Atlantic, 1959–60

———, *Free Jazz*, Atlantic, 1960

Coltrane, John, *Giant Steps*, Atlantic, 1959

———, *Kind Of Blue*, Columbia Jazz Masterpieces

———, *Live at the Village Vanguard*, MCA/Impulse, 1961

———, *A Love Supreme*, MCA/Impulse, 1964

———, *The Major Works of John Coltrane*, GRP/Impulse, 1965

Dolphy, Eric, *Out To Lunch*, Blue Note, 1964

Ibrahim, Abdullah (Dollar Brand), *African Piano*, ECM, 1969

Mingus, Charles, *Blues & Roots*, Atlantic, 1959

———, *Town Hall Concert 1964*, Fantasy/OJC, 1964

Monk, Thelonious, and John Coltrane, *Monk with Coltrane*, Fantasy/OJC, 1957

Sanders, Pharoah, *Tauhid*, Impulse

Shepp, Archie, *The Way Ahead*, Impulse

Taylor, Cecil, *Garden*, Hat Art 2, 1981

World Saxophone Quartet, *Steppin' With The World Saxophone Quartet*, Black Saint

The branching out of aesthetic streams and the recording explosion of the last thirty years make it impossible to supply an exhaustive listing for the last two chapters.

CHAPTER IV
THE ROAD TO CHANGE

On the Margins of History

Garner, Erroll, *Concert By The Sea*, Columbia Jazz Masterpieces, 1955

Peterson, Oscar, *The Trio*, Verve, 1961

————, *The Trio + 1*, Mercury, mid-1960s

Rollins, Sonny, *Saxophone Colossus*, Fantasy/OJC

Solal, Martial, *The RCA Sessions*, RCA

Bordering on Free Jazz

Ellis, Don, *How Time Passes*, Candid, 1960

Hancock, Herbie, *Maiden Voyage*, Blue Note

Henderson, Joe, *Inner Urge*, Blue Note, 1964

Hutcherson, Bobby, *Dialogue*, Blue Note, 1965

Little, Booker, *Outfront*, Candid, 1961

McLean, Jackie, *One Step Beyond*, Blue Note, 1963

Roach, Max, *We Insist: Freedom Now Suite*, Candid, 1960

Shorter, Wayne, *Speak No Evil*, Blue Note, 1964

————, *Juju*, Blue Note, 1964

Tyner, McCoy, *The Real McCoy*, Blue Note, 1967

Williams, Tony, *Lifetime*, Blue Note, 1964

From Bill Evans to the Miles Davis Quintet

Davis, Miles, *Cookin' At The Plugged Nickel*, Columbia Jazz Masterpieces, 1965

————, *Côte Blues (Live in Antibes)*, Jazz Music Yesterday, 1963

————, *Filles de Kilimanjaro*, Columbia Jazz Contemporary Masters, 1968

————, *Miles In The Sky*, Columbia, 1968

Evans, Bill, *Village Vanguard Sessions*, Milestone, 1961

————, *You Must Believe In Spring*, Warner Brothers

Evans, Bill, and Jim Hall, *Undercurrent*, Blue Note, 1962

The Advent Of Jazz-Rock

Brecker Brothers, *Heavy Metal Be-Bop*, Novus

Burton, Gary, *Gary Burton Quartet*, (with Larry Coryell and Steve Swallow), RCA, 1967

Corea, Chick, *No Mystery*, Polydor

Corea, Chick, Stanley Clarke, Flora Purim, et al., *Return To Forever*, ECM

Davis, Miles, *Agharta*, Columbia Jazz Contemporary Masters, 1975

————, *Bitches Brew*, Columbia Jazz Masterpieces, 1970

————, *In A Silent Way*, Columbia Jazz Masterpieces, 1969

Hancock, Herbie (The Head Hunters), *Head Hunters*, Columbia

McLaughlin, John (Mahavishnu Orchestra), *Birds of Fire*, Columbia, 1971–3

Weather Report, *Black Market*, Columbia

————, *Heavy Weather*, Columbia Jazz Contemporary Masters

————, *Mysterious Traveler*, Columbia

————, *Night Passage*, Columbia

The ECM Space (the passage from jazz-rock to a lighter music)

Abercrombie, John, *Gateway*, ECM, 1975

————, *Timeless*, ECM, 1974

Bley, Paul, *Open To Love*, ECM

Corea, Chick, and Gary Burton, *Crystal Silence*, ECM, 1972

Garbarek, Jan, and Bobo Stenson, *Dansere*, ECM

Gismonti, Egberto, *Sol Do Meio Dia*, ECM, 1977

Jarrett, Keith, *Facing You*, ECM, 1971

————, *The Survivor's Suite*, ECM, 1976

Jarrett, Keith, and Jan Garbarek, *Belonging*, ECM, 1974

Metheny, Pat, *Bright Size Life*, ECM, 1975

Surman, John, *Upon Reflection*, ECM

Towner, Ralph, *Solstice*, ECM, 1974

Wheeler, Kenny, *Deer Wan*, ECM, 1977

CHAPTER V
JAZZ BURSTS INTO PIECES

African-American Music

Blakey, Art, *Album Of The Year*, Timeless, 1981

Blanchard, Terence, and Donald Harrison, *Nascence*, Columbia

Coleman, Ornette, *Of Human Feelings*, Antilles, 1979

Coleman, Ornette, and Prime Time, *Virgin Beauty*, Portrait, 1988

Davis, Miles, *Decoy*, Columbia

————, *Tutu*, Warner Brothers, 1986

DeJohnette, Jack, *Album Album*, ECM, 1984

Coleman, Davis, and DeJohnette could all be godparents to:

Allen, Geri, *The Nurturer*, Blue Note, 1990

Coleman, Steve, *Rhythm In Mind*, Novus

Marsalis, Branford, *Random Abstract*, Columbia, 1987

Marsalis, Wynton, *Black Codes*, Columbia, 1985

Osby, Greg, *Man-Talk For Moderns*, Blue Note, 1990

Roberts, Marcus, *Deep In The Shed*, Novus, 1989

Thomas, Gary, *By Any Means Necessary*, Jazz Music Today

The Jazz Inheritance For White Musicians

Del Fra, Riccardo, *A Sip Of Your Touch*, IDA, 1989

Frisell, Bill, *Rambler*, ECM, 1984

———, *Is That You?*, Elektra/Musician, 1990

Keith Jarrett Trio, *Standards Live*, ECM, 1985

Johnson, Marc, and Bass Desires, *Bass Desires*, ECM, 1985

Kühn, Joachim, Daniel Humair, and Jean-François Jenny-Clark, *From Time To Time Free*, CMP, 1988

Liebman, David, and Richard Beirach, *Double Edge*, Storyville, 1985

Metheny, Pat, *Offramp*, ECM, 1981

Motian, Paul, *Monk in Motian*, Jazz Music Today, 1988

Peacock, Gary, *Guamba*, ECM, 1987

Romano, Aldo, *Ritual*, Owl

Scofield, John, *Meant To Be*, Blue Note, 1990

Writing for Moderate-Sized and Large Groups

Bley, Carla, *Social Studies*, ECM/Watt, 1980

Davis, Miles, *Aura*, Columbia, 1985

Evans, Gil, and Laurent Cugny (Lumiere Big Band), *Rhythm-A-Ning*, EmArcy, 1987

Pastorius, Jaco, *Word Of Mouth*, Warner Brothers

Russell, George, *New York Big Band*, Soul Note

———, *New York, N.Y.*, Decca Jazz

Vienna Art Orchestra, *Suite For The Green Eighties*, Hat Art 2, 1981

The Revolution of Musical Machines

Erskine, Peter, *Transition*, Denon, 1986

Louiss, Eddy, *Sang Mêlé*, Nocturne

Shorter, Wayne, *Atlantis*, Columbia

Steps Ahead, *Modern Times*, Elektra/Musician

Weather Report, *Sportin' Life*, Columbia, 1985

A Music of Fusion, in Every Sense of the Word

Fusion means musical recordings that are carefully put together in the studio, but it also designates the entire approach of contemporary jazz, which changes depending on the cultures it encounters.

Coe, Tony, *Les Voix d'Itxassou*, Nato

Diyici, Senem, *Takalar*, La Lichère

Doneda, Michel, *Terra*, Nato

Gonzalez, Jerry, *Rumba Para Monk*, Sunnyside

Goyone, Daniel, *Third Time*, Label Bleu

Hanrahan, Kip, *Days and Nights of Blue Luck Inverted*, American Clavé

Hussain, Zakir, *Making Music*, ECM

Hymas, Tony, *Oyaté*, Nato

Oregon, *Crossing*, ECM, 1973–84

Pascoal, Hermeto, *E Grupo*, Som Dagente

Ricos, André, and Louis Sclavis, *Le Partage des Eaux*, Silex

Sclavis, Louis, *Chine*, IDA, 1987

Sixun, *Explore*, Open

Temiz, Okay, and Sylvain Kassap, *Istanbul Da Eylül*, La Lichère

Ultramarine, *Dé*, Musidisc

Winstone, Norma, *Somewhere Called Home*, ECM, 1986

Yamamoto, Hozan, *Silver World*, Philips

Further Reading

Balliett, Whitney, *New York Notes: A Journal of Jazz in the Seventies*, Houghton Mifflin, Boston, 1976

————, *Night Creature: A Journal of Jazz, 1975–80*, Oxford University Press, New York, 1981

Berendt, Joachim, *The Jazz Book: From Ragtime to Fusion and Beyond*, Chicago Review Press, Chicago, 1982

Carr, Ian, *Miles Davis: A Biography*, William Morrow, New York, 1982

Chambers, Jack, *Milestones One: The Music and Times of Miles Davis to 1960*, William Morrow, New York, 1985

————, *Milestones Two: The Music and Times of Miles Davis Since 1960*, William Morrow, New York, 1985

Coker, Jerry, *The Jazz Idiom*, Prentice-Hall, Englewood Cliffs, New Jersey, 1975

Cole, Bill, *John Coltrane*, Schirmer, New York, 1976

Collier, James Lincoln, *The Making of Jazz: A Comprehensive History*, Houghton Mifflin, Boston, 1978

Coryell, Julie, and Laura Friedman, *Jazz-Rock Fusion: The People, the Music*, Delacorte Press, New York, 1978

Dance, Stanley, *The World of Count Basie*, Scribner's, New York, 1980

Davis, Miles, and Quincy Troupe, *Miles, the Autobiography*, Simon & Schuster, New York, 1989

Feather, Leonard, *Encyclopedia of Jazz in the Sixties*, Bonanza Books, New York, 1966

————, *The Passion for Jazz*, Horizon Press, New York, 1980

————, *The Pleasures of Jazz*, Horizon Press, New York, 1976

Feather, Leonard, and Ira Gitler, *Encyclopedia of Jazz in the Seventies*, Horizon Press, New York, 1976

Gillespie, Dizzy, and Al Fraser, *To Be or Not to Bop: Memoirs of Dizzy Gillespie*, Da Capo Press, 1979

Gleason, Ralph, *Celebrating the Duke...and Other Heroes*, Little, Brown and Co., Boston, 1975

Gottlieb, William P., *The Golden Age of Jazz*, Simon & Schuster, New York, 1979

Harrison, Max, *A Jazz Retrospect*, Crescendo Publishing Co., Boston, 1976

Hentoff, Nat, *Jazz Is*, Random House, New York, 1976

Hodeir, André, *Toward Jazz*, Da Capo, New York, 1976

Kofsky, Frank, *Black Nationalism and the Revolution in Music*, Pathfinder, New York, 1970

Lyons, Leonard, *The Great Jazz Pianists*, Da Capo, New York, 1989

Mingus, Charles, *Beneath the Underdog*, Knopf, New York, 1971

Nisenson, Eric, *'Round About Midnight: A Portrait of Miles Davis*, Dial, New York, 1982

Pepper, Art, and Laurie Pepper, *Straight Life: The Story of Art Pepper*, Schirmer, New York, 1979

Reisner, Robert G., *Bird: The Legend of Charlie Parker*, Bonanza, New York, 1962

Russell, George, *The Lydian Chromatic Concept of Tonal Organization*, Concept, New York, 1953

Russell, Ross, *Bird Lives! The High Life and Hard Times of Charlie Parker*, Charterhouse, New York, 1973

Simon, George T., et al., *The Best of the Music Makers*, Doubleday, New York, 1979

Simpkins, C. O., *Coltrane: A Biography*, Herndon House, New York, 1975

Spellman, A. B., *Black Music: Four Lives*, Schocken, New York, 1970

Thomas, J. C., *Chasin' the Trane: The Music and Mystique of John Coltrane*, Doubleday, Garden City, New York, 1975

Ullmann, Michael, *Jazz Lives*, New Republic Books, Washington, D.C., 1980

List of Illustrations

Index

Acknowledgments

The authors and publishers would like to thank Pascal Anquetil, Claude Carrière, and Alain Tercinet

Photograph Credits

Text Credits

Grateful acknowledgment is made for use of material from the following: Chambers, Jack, *Milestones I: The Music and Times of Miles Davis to 1960*, University of Toronto Press, 1983. Copyright © Jack Chambers. Used by permission of the author (pp. 116, 118). Davis, Miles, and Quincy Troupe, *Miles, the Autobiography*, New York, Simon & Schuster, Inc. Copyright © 1989 Miles Davis. Reprinted by permission of Simon & Schuster, Inc. (pp. 115–6, 116–8, 128–9, 136–7). Gillespie, Dizzy, *To Be or Not to Bop*, New York, Doubleday. Copyright © 1979 by John Birks Gillespie and Wilmot Alfred Fraser. Used by permission of Doubleday, a division of Bantam Doubleday Dell Publishing Group, Inc. (pp. 120–3)

Franck Bergerot was born in 1953. Although he has a passion for several different forms of popular music, he has devoted himself to the most erudite, jazz. He has written for *Jazz Hot* and *Monde de la Musique* and teaches the history of jazz at the University of Paris X. In 1990 he directed the recording of the anthology *Paris-Musette*, which won the Grand Prix du Disque of the Académie Charles-Cros in France.

Arnaud Merlin was born in Tours, France, in 1963. After studying music at the Sorbonne and at the Conservatoire National Supérieur de Musique de Paris, he became a journalist. He is a contributor to *Jazz Hot, Jazz à Paris, Monde de la Musique,* and *France-Musique.* He is co-author of *L'Agenda du Jazz* (1989) and *Jazz en France.*

Translated from the French by Marjolijn de Jager

Project Manager: Sharon AvRutick
Typographic Designer: Robert McKee
Editorial Assistant: Jennifer Stockman
Design Assistant: Penelope Hardy
Text Permissions: Neil Ryder Hoos

Library of Congress Catalog Card Number: 92–82804

ISBN 0–8109–2876–0

Copyright © 1991 Gallimard

English translation copyright © 1993 Harry N. Abrams, Inc., New York, and Thames and Hudson Ltd., London

Published in 1993 by Harry N. Abrams, Incorporated, New York

Printed and bound in Italy by Editoriale Libraria, Trieste